Tatina A. Cowell

I Feel Like a Poem

Wider Perspectives Publishing ¤ 2024 ¤ Hampton Roads, Va.

The poems and writings in this book are the creations and property of Tatina Cowell, the author is responsible for them as such. Wider Perspectives Publishing reserves 1st run rights to this material in this form, all rights revert to author upon delivery. Author reserves all rights thereafter: Do not reproduce, distribute or transmit without Author's written permission except Fair Use practices for approved promotion or educational purposes. Author may redistribute, whole or in part, at will, for example submission to anthologies or contests.

© 2023, Tatina A. Cowell
1st run complete in January 2024
Wider Perspectives Publishing, Hampton Roads, Va.
ISBN 978-1-952773-85-3

A Collection of my Humanity Expressed Through Poetry

Tatina A. Cowell

Dedicated to those who persevere...
To those who keep going despite the test and the trials...
Dedicated to my Angels...
We win!

Contents

YOUR WORDS FEEL LIKE:
FOREWORD BY AUTHOR & POET,
DONESSA ARAPI

I FEEL LIKE INTRODUCING MYSELF
(INTRODUCTORY POEM)   1

part I   I FEEL LIKE CHAOS & PAIN   5

part II   I FEEL LIKE SEX   43

part III   I FEEL LIKE LOVE   63

part IV   I FEEL LIKE WORSHIP   91

    A WORD OF THANKS   129

    ABOUT THE AUTHOR   130

Your words feel like...

YOUR WORDS ARE BEAUTIFUL. THEY PENETRATE THE MIND AND HEART WITH A HARMONIOUS FLOW THAT INTRIGUES THE READER. YOU HAVE A NATURAL ABILITY TO TRANSFORM THOUGHTS TO WORDS AND WORDS INTO AN IMAGE, WHICH TAKES YOUR READERS ON AN EMOTIONAL JOURNEY THROUGH YOU AND ALLOWING THEM TO PARTAKE IN A VISION OF THEIR OWN. YOU ARE GIFTED AND VERY TALENTED. YOUR SOUL IS DEEP AND RICH WITH SEED. YOU ARE DESTINED TO PROVOKE THOUGHT. YOU ARE GIFTED TO REACH DOWN AND REVEAL THE SPIRIT INSIDE. YOU ARE CHARGED WITH BEING A VOICE TO THOSE WHO BELIEVE THAT THEY ARE ALONE AND THAT NO-ONE UNDERSTANDS THEIR PLIGHT, THEIR PASSION OR THEM AS A PERSON...THANK YOU FOR SHARING, I APPRECIATE THE OPPORTUNITY TO READ AND LEARN FROM YOUR WORK.

- Donessa Arapi, Author and Poet

I Feel Like ...
Introducing Myself

*Ask me who I am, and I will say
that I am complexed.*

I Feel Like A Poem (Introductory Poem)

I FEEL LIKE A POEM...

I FEEL LIKE GRAVITY PULLED BACK
SOARING HIGH INTO THE SKY
I FEEL LIKE SCATTERED PIECES
    TO A PUZZLE BEGGING TO CONNECT
I FEEL LIKE I'M AN IMBECILE
TEACHING A CLASS OF INTELLECTUALS
LEADING THEM INTO AN EVOLUTIONARY WAR
AGAINST WHAT HAS BEEN LABELED AS THE NORM
I FEEL LIKE TRUE WORSHIP TEARING DOWN THE WALLS
OF SYSTEMATIC RELIGION AND INSTITUTIONALIZATION
I FEEL LIKE I'M A DEMONSTRATION...
OF FREEDOM
I FEEL LIKE ART, ABSTRACT AND COLORFUL
UNPREDICTABLE
I FEEL LIKE I'M A LITTLE MYSTICAL
ABSORBED BY THE GLORY OF WHAT IS SPIRITUAL
I FEEL LIKE THE SOUL TIES
LACED BETWEEN MY THIGHS
AS MY NATURE STARTS TO RISE
YET I FIGHT CONSTANTLY NOT TO COMPROMISE
I FEEL LIKE THE BEGINNING
WHEN EVERYTHING WAS NEW AND
THERE WAS NO SUCH THING AS AN ENDING

I FEEL LIKE A POEM...

A Collection of My Humanity Expressed Through Poetry

I FEEL LIKE THE LIE THAT YOU TAUGHT ME
THAT I HAVE TWO NAMES
OF BEING A NOTHING, AND A NOBODY
I FEEL LIKE TIME SPENT WASTED
WATCHING DREAMS FADE INTO NIGHT TERRORS
AND THE ONLY ERROR
WAS MY IN-EFFORT TO MOVE BEYOND THE FEARS

I FEEL LIKE THE FALLING TEARS
THAT NEVER SEEM TO STOP
FORCED BY THE VIOLENT POP
OF ANOTHER COP'S GUNSHOT
I FEEL LIKE WORDS THAT WILL NEVER CEASE
I FEEL LIKE A VESSEL LIVING IN SEARCH OF A RELEASE
I FEEL LIKE A MIND ARRESTED
    IN JUVENILE DELINQUENCY
MY THOUGHTS MIX LIKE THE BEATS VARYING
    IN MUSICAL FREQUENCIES
I FEEL LIKE A PASSAGE
ENCODED WITH THE MESSAGE THAT I AM
    THE RESURRECTED
I GUESS I JUST FEEL LIKE WHAT I FEEL LIKE...

I FEEL LIKE A POEM.

I WELCOME YOU TO ME. - *TATINA*

Tatina A. Cowell

I Feel Like a Poem

A Collection of My Humanity Expressed Through Poetry

PART I

I Feel Like ...

Chaos & Pain

*A person divided into multiple halves,
fragments, and fractions,
yet solely expressed in a singular voice.*

*The sad thing is,
Sometimes it feels normal to feel this way.
Like I am nothing. Can you hear me?*

Tatina A. Cowell

I Feel Like a Poem

A Simple Plea

I AM FORCED TO BE SILENT
IN FEAR THAT YOU WILL BECOME ANGRY
AND BANISH ME.
AND SO MY HEART IS AN EXPLOSION
IMPRISONED BY ISOLATION,
TORMENTED BY MISUNDERSTANDING
AND NONACCEPTANCE.
BUT MAY I PLEASE SPEAK
WITH ONE SIMPLE REQUEST…
LOVE ME

Buried

Perfection is a dream that we create
A fallacy within itself
Just as I am a sponge
soaking up the earth's soil,
stricken with pain and abuse
that I don't know how to release
Hurt just seems so natural to me
I'm accustomed to being used
then cast by the wayside
Laid away without claim or full payment
Never to become wholly yours
but left abandoned and empty
Begging to be filled with more than
just your baggage
I have my own that I can't contain anymore
It swallows me whole, suffocating
I'm trying to breathe but the boulders
just keep falling
Burying me alive

Cycles

It's become more difficult
to just be... To smile
Every thought is full of emptiness
and if it's not empty it's dark...
And tiring
My imagination is short of breath
and life is barely a thing worth having
I found myself here before
and I can't seem to figure out
how this cycle starts,
ends,
and then it begins...
Again.

Hidden

I'M FULL
THE ONLY THING I CAN SAY
NOT KNOWING WHAT TO FEEL FIRST
SADNESS
PAIN
ANXIETY
LUST
LOVE
PRESSURE
FEAR
EXCITEMENT
DEPRESSION
BROKENNESS
GRIEF BEYOND GRIEF
HOW CAN I PROCESS WHAT I CAN'T CLEARLY IDENTIFY?
EVERYTHING COMING AT A FULL CIRCLE
RAPIDLY SPINNING
AROUND AND AROUND
AROUND AND AROUND
AND AROUND AGAIN
WHAT AM I SUPPOSED TO DO?
I FEEL LIKE I WANT TO FOLD UP IN A CORNER
AND JUST STAY THERE…
HIDDEN AWAY FROM THIS WORLD
SOMETIMES, I THINK IT WOULD EVEN BE
EASIER IF I COULD HIDE FROM MYSELF

Burn

I STAND OUTSIDE OF MYSELF
WATCHING MYSELF SET YOU ON FIRE
I GRIN HOPING THAT YOU'RE EXPERIENCING
A SMIDGE OF THE PAIN YOU LEFT ME IN
WATCHING YOUR SKIN BOIL
AS YOU FEEL THE BURN
THAT CAUSED MY HEART TO MELT INTO
BRITTLE PIECES RESEMBLING ASH.

YOU WANTED TO KNOW HOW REJECTION FEELS
WELL, IT SORT OF LIKE THE SENSATION
AS YOU CRY OUT LONGING FOR THE ICE COLD
CHILL OF RESCUE, YET THE ONLY THING LEFT
IS THE COLDNESS OF MY INNER SHELL
EXONERATED BY YOUR AGONY
IN THIS MOMENT WHEN YOU NEED IT THE MOST...

I KNOW YOU'D LIKE AN EXTINGUISHER
BUT I'D RATHER EXTINGUISH YOU

Codes

I speak in codes
hoping you'd
decipher the true meaning
laid beneath the surface
Subliminal messages
encrypted by withdrawal
and round about speech
purposely drafted to
hide the way I feel.
Sarcastic tweets
hinting at my rage
For nothing giggles
illustrating my endearment
toward you
Anonymous poetry
scribed on the walls of
Social media exhibits the
informal lingo of my heart
with random posts and pics
depicting my most inward thoughts
But still, you have not a clue
And so I paint a picture
of a bleeding heart
pierced with a dagger
a slightly angled horseshoe
swaying at the tip
portraying a version of 'u'
...of me...of you and me
playing back and forth in riddles

I Feel Like a Poem

OF UNEXPRESSED EMOTIONS
PHOTOGRAPHS OF YOUR SMILE
AS I FLIP THROUGH MENTAL ALBUMS
REMEMBERING EVERY REASON
WHY YOU ARE INSTILLED IN ME...
BUT I REFUSE TO CALL
BELIEVING YOUR HEART WILL GROW
FONDER IN MY ABSENCE
I PULL AWAY TO WATCH
AS BLURRED LINES COME INTO FOCUS
NO MORE AM I TRUSTING IN WORDS
LEFT UNSAID, INSTEAD
I TRUST IN WHAT
YOU HAVE MADE CLEAR
THAT OUR LOVE LANGUAGE IS UNCOMMON
AND THERE IS NO NEED TO CONTINUE
OUR SPEECH IN CODE

A Collection of My Humanity Expressed Through Poetry

The Black Hole

Dismal and lost, never knowing
where to go or who to turn to,
so I disappear within myself,
creating this false place of security
this internal fortress that keeps me crippled,
afraid to move outward into the light
It consumes me...
This black hole
     known as life
     or at least this fictitious
     representation of one
Yet how do I walk ahead into
     the surrounding space
where illumination and peace reside, instead
of this dark pit of desolation
     and internal horror
I've allowed myself to entertain in my mind
I don't want to linger in this process,
but I can't find my place of promise,
a land flowing with milk
and honey...
I need to make my escape
out of this Bermuda Triangle where fear, hurt,
and stagnation hold me captive
Can someone turn on the light,
or at least help me to find the switch?
Grab hold of my hand, somebody, anybody...
Whoever is standing on the outside,
and please, pull me out of this black hole

Tatina A. Cowell

I Feel Like a Poem

The Coat

I WEAR A HAPPY FACE
THE WAY A TRENCH COAT
PERFECTLY FITS YOUR FRAME
TO COVER EVERY CUT, BRUISE AND SCAR
YOU MASQUERADE AS POISED AND
CONFIDENT, YET BENEATH IS TORMENT...
BROKENNESS

YOU LIE WIDE OPEN FOR
EVERYONE TO SEE, AND YET
THE ONLY ONE BLIND IS YOU
AS YOU'VE CHOSEN TO REMAIN
A MYSTERY TO YOURSELF
A LITTLE GIRL WHO CRIES INSIDE HER
SECRET CLOSET CONTEMPLATING DEATH.

I KNOW THAT YOU'RE LONELY.
I UNDERSTAND.
I TOLD YOU I WEAR HAPPY
THE SAME WAY YOU WEAR A COAT
TO KEEP YOU COZY AND COMFORTABLE,
BUT SOMEHOW THE CHILL CONTINUES
TO CREEP IN, EVEN SLIGHTLY,
THROUGH THE NEAREST CRACK
YOU SENSE THE BREEZE,
SPREADING TO MAKE YOU FEEL NUMB
TO FEELING NOTHING.

BUT I WEAR THE SMILE
JUST AS YOU WEAR THE COAT
BECAUSE NO ONE TRULY CARES
TO ASK YOU HOW YOU FEEL
AS LONG AS THEY STAY WARM.

I Feel Like a Poem

His Name is D

He was dark and mysterious
Always welcoming
He whispered phrases
that spoke to my senses
as he stood close to me,
sinking deep
into my consciousness
Alluring to the shadows
of my heart
that seemed ignored by most
He reconciled my deficiencies
as I was unstable in my way of thinking
I am always alone.
My inside torn, drenching
wet in the dismal swamps
left by torrential rains
and gusting rapids winds of sin
Yet he wants me, he calls me consistently
I must say, he's persistent.
In an enlightened tone
he requests my presence
Lay with me he asks, and not temporarily
but for eternity I want to console you
totally, and whole. He pauses.
Please forgive me for being rude
as I have failed to introduce myself.
You can call me D,
though most know me as Death
Lurking, and lingering,

A Collection of My Humanity Expressed Through Poetry

OBSERVING YOUR PAIN THAT
I AM OFFERING A RELEASE.
SO, VISIT ME IN NEVERLAND
AND YOU WILL NEVER AGAIN
KNOW A SINGLE DRIP, DROP OR DRIZZLE
OF LIFE'S MENACING STORMS
THEY SAY I'M COLD,
YET I'M HERE
AND MY ARMS ARE ALWAYS OPEN
SO REST NEXT TO ME
AND I WILL MAKE YOU WARM
I CAN FEEL MYSELF
GETTING WEAK AND HIS SMILE IS
SO GENTLE. BLUE SKIES START TO TURN GRAY
BUT THEY DON'T MAKE ME SAD
THEY MAKE ME FEEL WELCOME
LIKE I'M GOING HOME TO MOM'S
HOMEMADE SWEET POTATO PIE
AND I WON'T LIE...I WANT TO GO
FAR AWAY FROM HERE
WHERE LIFE JUST SEEMS HARD
WEIGHTED DOWN AND FACES OF LOVE
LOOK MORE LIKE SPOILED PAINTINGS
OF COLORS FADING OFF OF THE CANVASES
THAT WERE MEANT TO HOLD IT CLOSE.
WHERE ARE YOU D?
'CAUSE I'M STILL HERE
IN THE LIVING, BARELY LIVING...
RELEASE ME.

Tatina A. Cowell

Guarantee

I could tell you
exactly how I feel, but
I can guarantee
you couldn't handle it

You couldn't handle my questions
or my mistrust in God
Instead, you'll just keep reaffirming
that it all works together for my good

You couldn't handle my choice
to no longer struggle in how I feel
or who I love
You couldn't handle my choice to just be
in effort to understand
His grace and love in place of
the bondage, condemnation
subconsciously instilled in me

You couldn't handle
my anger, my rage
You couldn't handle this roar I'm trying
to suppress in an effort to stand on
the side of right even when right
just feels so fucking wrong

I COULD TELL YOU
EXACTLY HOW I FEEL, BUT
I CAN GUARANTEE
YOU COULDN'T HANDLE IT

HOWEVER, I CAN GUARANTEE THIS...
I CAN GUARANTEE THE AWKWARD STARES
THE SILENT JUDGMENT
I COULD GUARANTEE YOU DECIDING WHO I AM
BASED ON THESE WORDS AS OPPOSED TO
THE HEART YOU MET YEARS AGO BEFORE
THE PAIN INTRODUCED ITSELF INTO MY LIFE

I COULD GUARANTEE
THAT YOU CAN'T HANDLE
THE PERSON I AM NOW
VERSUS THE PERSON YOU BOXED INTO
THIS IMAGERY BEFORE THE EVOLUTION
I CAN GUARANTEE THAT WHILE YOU WANTED
ME TO STAY THE SAME, THIS JOURNEY
SPOKE DIFFERENT

I CAN GUARANTEE THAT MY STORY
IS BEING CONTINUED
MY ARC BEING DEVELOPED
CHAPTERS STILL TO BE WRITTEN
REVELATIONS YET TO BE UNVEILED

I Feel Like a Poem

BUT I CAN ALSO GUARANTEE THAT
IF TELL YOU EXACTLY, HOW I FEEL,
EVEN AFTER ALL OF THIS,
YOU STILL JUST PROBABLY COULDN'T HANDLE IT

He'll Listen

My insides are spilling over
but I have no idea what to do
Pray?
I can't trust that to be the answer
so, I ask those I love and
who I trust to love me
to send up a word
Maybe He'll listen to you
because I'm tired of dealing
in this feeling
of being ignored

Am I not listening close enough?
Is the message being intercepted?
Is the transmission malfunctioning?

Static and silence prevail
while the inquiries proceed to excel
I'm tired of consistently
persistently
picking straws in weighty haystacks
It's like racing toward that pot
at the end of the rainbow
yet the colors fade
before I reach the gold
and I'm getting to a point of
my belief being sold

Your advice...

Pray?

But I just can't trust that to be the answer
So, I ask those I love and
who I trust to love me
to send up a word
I think maybe He'll listen to you

Pearly Whites

I pat myself on the back
whenever I can muster up
the strength to smile

Looks can be deceiving
and it's not easy
I mean, the facade is real
but I do what I need
to get through the day

The next conversation,
polite gestures,
greetings,
oftentimes accompanied with a hug,
a cheerful wave across the room...
My jokes and laugh
come from a place where
without you knowing,
laughter and heartwarming
have been pushed aside
by their rivals,
pissed off and tired

It's like my Gemini
I choose to leave at home
pouty on the couch,
wanting to break free
so she can break free

I Feel Like a Poem

AND BREAK SOME THINGS
BUT I CAN'T LET HER OUT
CAUSE THAT JUST MAY COST ME
MORE THAN I'M READY
AND/OR WILLING TO PAY
SO, I'LL JUST SMILE
I'LL JUST SIT IN THE STATE I'M IN
HIDING BEHIND THESE PERFECTLY
CRAFTED STONE WALLS
WHILE MY PEARLY WHITES
REMAIN EXPOSED
FOR YOUR DELIGHT

A Collection of My Humanity Expressed Through Poetry

Tatina A. Cowell

I Feel Like a Poem

Insignificant

I KNOW THAT YOU'RE NOT INTERESTED
BUT PLEASE, DON'T TREAT ME AS IF
MY FEELINGS ARE INSIGNIFICANT

YOU DON'T REALIZE
THE PORTRAITS OF YOU AND I
MY WILLINGNESS TO SCAR MY PRIDE
SO WE CAN RIDE OR DIE, TOGETHER
TO BE MORE THAN SIMPLY FRIENDS
CAUSE I'M TRYING TO BE THE LENS
THAT SEARCHES DEEP INTO YOUR SOUL
I'VE BEEN LONGING TO CONSOLE
THE DISTRUST THAT YOUR HEART STILL BEHOLDS
ATTEMPTING TO BE CLOSER THAN THE CLOSE,
YET YOU BLOCK YOUR EARS
SO YOU CAN'T HEAR VERY CLEAR
MY HEART THAT BEATS FOR YOU
AS I IMAGINE THE TASTE OF YOUR LIPS
AS MOIST AS THE MORNING DEW

AND THOUGH YOU'RE NOT INTERESTED,
JUST PLEASE DON'T TREAT ME AS IF
MY FEELINGS ARE INSIGNIFICANT

AT FIRST, I KIND OF THOUGHT IT WAS DOPE
THE WAY YOU HELPED ME
CREATE THIS FALSE HOPE
OF A POSSIBILITY OF US BUILDING
A DUAL ABILITY TO MEET IN THIS

Symphonic harmony
of feminine blends
And I don't want this mental affair to end
When you smile is where I begin
To see you...
Sometimes, a hardened wall,
yet beneath it you care
I'm looking for just a glare
and I can't help but stare,
I keep trying to figure you out,
yet all I run into are these circles of doubt
Because I know that you're not interested,
but I beg, please don't treat me
as if my feelings are insignificant.

I Feel Like a Poem

Just Enough

Someone I hold dear to me said at one time
That tears are for the weak
I believe the contrary to be true
Tears are a sign of morality,
Exposing man's ability to feel...
Man's ability to love...
Man's ability to push self aside
And place another man ahead.

Tears have become a personal outlet
When I think of that friend who once told me
That tears are a call for pity.

To that friend, I'd tell them that
I've shed tears for the burdens you carry
And for the burdens I've allowed myself to
carry with you.

To that friend, I'd tell them of my tears of anger
And my tears that plead to erase the resentment
Because of the uncertainty of
Knowing if you are truly my friend...

But maybe that is the case...
I am your friend, but you are not mine
So my tears rooted in bitterness and hurt are
actually
My tears of denial, refusing to accept that
You really do not love me.

THE TRUTH IS, NO MATTER WHO THE PERSON MAY BE
OR THEIR PLACE IN OUR HEARTS, FACING THE
REALIZATION THAT SOMEONE YOU LOVE
DOESN'T LOVE YOU BACK IS JUST ENOUGH
TO MAKE ANYONE CRY.

I Feel Like a Poem

Lonely, I Heard

Lonely, I heard...
I heard your voice
in the body that didn't lay
next to me at night
I heard you when there were
no arms to uphold me when I cry
or to tell me
everything would be alright

I heard you in a room, where
I stood center, surrounded
by a crowd that didn't even
notice me, yet I smiled pretending
I was with somebody
but the only presence near
was a chivalrous gentleman
named Nobody is here
but Lonely, I heard...

I heard you in the mixed
messages that people send,
in the mixed messages in which they tend
to believe that they love you emphatically,
and of course, through words, I mean, that's easy,
but too selfish to show forth the action
and then they expect your reaction
to be an open arms welcoming view
of round two of them neglecting you
but Lonely, I heard...

I HEARD YOU IN A TIME WHEN IMAGINATION
RAN WILD WITH NEW IDEAS AND SPONTANEOUS
CONCEPTS OF HOW WE COULD BE
AND EVEN THOUGH I WOULD BLEED INWARDLY
I COULD STILL SEE INTO THE CHILDLIKE IMAGERY
OF LIVING LIFE BEYOND THESE MEDIOCRE THINGS

LONELY, I HEARD…

I HEARD YOU WHEN YOU SHARED YOUR VISION,
AND IT SEEMED AS IF NO ONE LISTENED
THE ONES WHO STOOD NEXT TO YOU
DIDN'T GET IT, AND SO THEY DISMISSED IT
AND THEN YOU HID IT

LONELY, I HEARD
THAT YOUR HEART WAS BROKEN
AND ALL THE WHILE,
FOLK STILL EXPECTED YOU TO SMILE
AS IF YOUR SOUL DIDN'T WALK SLOW
DOWN THAT GREEN MILE

I HEARD YOU LONELY WHEN THEY ASKED
IF YOU WERE PASS THE PAST, AND SO YOU ATTEMPT
TO MOVE PASS THE PAST FAST, HOPING THAT
THE PERSISTENT RIDICULE WON'T LAST
BUT LONELY, I HEARD

I Feel Like a Poem

I HEARD YOU WONDERING IF YOU WERE
THE ONLY ONE WHO LIVES LIKE YOU, THINKS LIKE YOU
SPEAKS LIKE YOU, THE ONLY ONE WHO... LOVES LIKE YOU
I HEAR YOU LONELY

I HEARD YOU WHEN THERE WERE MORE QUESTIONS
THAN ANSWERS, AND YOU TRY TO AVOID THE BANTER
OF EXPRESSING PHONY FLATTER AND THE ONLY THING
THAT MATTERED WAS FIGHTING TO KEEP YOUR LAUGHTER
LONELY, I HEARD YOU

I HEARD YOUR FRANTIC TONE
IN PANIC WHEN IT SEEMED
EVERYONE FLED, INSTANTLY GONE
THEN I HEARD YOU WHEN YOU WHISPERED,
PLEASE, DON'T LEAVE...I'M BEGGING
I JUST DON'T WANT TO BE LEFT ALONE
LONELY, I HEARD

Obsession

You've become my obsession
erecting every neurotic
imagery in my membrane
I think I'm insane
with these constant rotations
of your dialect igniting
my mental stimuli
I let you in too deep
to the point that
I can't even sleep
I'm awakened by your voice
this persistent noise
longing, hoping you'd fill this void
I'm empty. I'm limping.
Chasing after your silhouette
And I'm getting wet
and then you suddenly disappear
and I'm just wishing that you'd reappear
so I can consume you
And maybe this is just my imagination
my fascination
I'm infatuated… with you
A connection that exist only in my mind
And I'm trying to find
a means to erase this line
that standing between us.

I Feel Like a Poem

Out of Touch

I CRY
TRYING TO REMEMBER
WHAT IT FELT LIKE
TO BE TOUCHED
AN EMBRACE
JUST FEELS SO DISTANT
AND OUT OF REACH
CAN YOU, WILL YOU
LAY YOUR HANDS ON ME?
AND I'M NOT TALKING SEX,
BUT A CONNECTION
AFFECTION...
SOME RESEMBLANCE OF LOVE
IN RELATION TO REALITY
DON'T STARVE ME
BY KEEPING ME OUT OF REACH
OUT OF TOUCH
SOMETHING THAT I NEED SO MUCH
IS A HUG TOO MUCH TO ASK
A KISS ON THE CHEEK
A SHOULDER TO REST MY HEAD
OH! BUT YOU DON'T HAVE TIME...
TO LOVE
TO FEEL
TO INDULGE
THE NECESSITY TO BE NEAR
YOU'VE BECOME ONLY
ACCUSTOMED TO SPACE

AND CLOSENESS
IS AN IMAGINED THING
ALTHOUGH, IT FELT REAL TO ME.

I Feel Like a Poem

The Main Question

My niece died unprotected
My sister left not loving herself
My mom lost her quality of life
with her last breath
given not from where it came
but given over to machines
See my life isn't the same,
It's actually opposes
what I once believed...
The ways I've been taught
Maybe it's anger speaking?
Sadness, frustration
Disappointment
Hell, all of the above
I mean what do You expect?
I've been taught a lot
Most I've tried to follow
yet it left me feeling more tied and bond...
Different from how I see myself now
no longer pretending
that the jargon works, or
emulating behaviors that haven't really
instilled in me change
I mean, what do You expect?
Teach me Your way,
but can You grant me evidence?
Not just lingo spoken by sheep
living, walking these hypocritical steps

WHO CAN TRULY UNDERSTAND
THE STRIFE IN ME?
THE CHANGE AND THE TRAUMA
THE VOIDS, BRUISES, AND SCARS
IN MY HONESTY, AM I BEING BLASPHEMOUS?
IN MY SEEKING A RELATIONSHIP
GROUNDED IN TRUTH WITH YOU
CAN I BE TOTALLY HONEST?
IS IT OKAY TO BE REAL?
THE ELDERS ALWAYS TOLD ME
TO NEVER ASK GOD WHY?
THE THING IS,
THAT'S THE MAIN QUESTION
I HAVE.

Tatina A. Cowell

I Feel Like a Poem

The Reality Behind The Mask

I laugh to cover up the anguish
while all along your presumption of me
is actually in opposition of the reality
I am a figment of your imagination
one sculpted and molded out of my observation
to fit in with your expectation
You seem surprised by this revelation
when in fact it has been said that a frown
is simply smile turned upside down,
though in my circumstance
I prefer that you not turn it around
Have you ever considered this,
the idea of my disposition
or the character you have come to know
maybe an illusion created
    to blind you from the hurt
and hostility of a bitter past I fail to let go?
Can you even imagine your present form
    as a building
and living within your walls is a child,
    who cries herself to sleep,
fantasizing of being someone other than herself
due to wounds laid deep?
Well, this is the lie that I have lived to please you
A single shell of one person divided into
    multiples of two
Happiness is the mask I wear to hide away my tears
so that you won't consider me weak,

A Collection of My Humanity Expressed Through Poetry

WITNESSING ALL OF MY FRAILTIES AND FEARS
YET IN FACT I AM A PERSON, WHO HAS BEEN BROKEN,
    NOT IN HALF,
BUT IN MANY PIECES TIED TO SOULS
    SCATTERED IN THE DISTANT
AND YOU DARE TO QUESTION THE ORIGIN
    OF MY RESENTMENT
I SEARCH WITHIN MYSELF FOR A SMILE THAT IS GENUINE
AND NOT SIMPLY A FALSE, DECEPTIVE REPLICATION OF ME
BUT WHO AM I? BECAUSE I DON'T KNOW –
    OR AM I MERELY CAST AWAY AT SEA
SOMEWHERE MY IDENTITY GOT LOST
    IN YOUR IMPRESSIONS
AND FORGIVE ME BECAUSE IT WAS NEVER MY INTENTION
    TO ENCOURAGE YOUR MISPERCEPTIONS
BUT I DID TO PLEASE YOU…
I DID SO THAT YOU WOULD NOT LEAVE ME,
    YET STILL YOU DID
LEAVE ME CRYING, BRUISED AND BLEEDING
BECAUSE WHAT I THOUGHT TO BE LOVE
    WAS TRULY MISLEADING
NOW I REALIZE I CANNOT AFFORD FOR THIS
MASQUERADE TO LAST
BUT IN ORDER FOR ME TO BE FREE, I MUST EXPOSE
THE REALITY BEHIND THE MASK
THEREFORE, OPENLY I WEEP, CONFESSING ALL OF MY SINS
WITH A MINDSET FOUNDED ON HOPE THAT THIS AGONY
WILL SOON COME TO AN END

Tatina A. Cowell

I Feel Like a Poem

While your opinions may change
    and you assume me to be soft,
at this point in my life, I do not care
    because it is time
for me to take the mask off

Turmoil

Looking for answers
But all I run into are these dark dead ends
Inwardly, it's like an eruption that I fight
to hold back, but for how long can an individual
implode as opposed to explode?

Anxiety, worry…esteem so low
Circles of trust versus the mistrust
It's a scattered puzzle with no absolute
directory toward completion,
But where is the assurance of mental stability
instead of walking around
on this constantly shaky ground?

I feel like it's the enemy is tempting me
to say that I'm crazy…that I'm going insane
But if I profess damnation
Then I hinder my own elevation
Of reaching God's true revelation
Of His designation appointed for my life…
Though I won't pretend,
that my spirit isn't in strife

Sometimes, I want to die, but I can't…
Simply for the fact that He won't let me
So then I attempt to figure out how exactly am
I suppose to live?

I Feel Like a Poem

MY MIND LOADED UP ON BUILDING BLOCKS
    WITH NO LETTERS
COUNTLESS BLANK SPOTS...
COUNTLESS BLANK SPOTS...
WHEN SUDDENLY THE ANSWER APPEARS FOR ME TO BE...
TO SIMPLY REST IN HIS REST

AH! IT'S A SIGH OF RELIEF...
THE COMPLICATIONS, THEY GRADUALLY DISAPPEAR
THE COAST STARTS TO BECOME A LITTLE MORE CLEAR
    FOR ME
NO LONGER AM I LOST INSIDE OF THIS FANTASY,
WHICH IS MORE LIKE A NIGHTMARE WHERE THE ENEMY
IS STRIVING TO ROB ME OF ME
BUT, I GUESS WHAT I'M FINALLY TRYING TO SAY IS,
FAREWELL TO YOU, TURMOIL.

A Collection of My Humanity Expressed Through Poetry

PART II

I Feel Like …

*Urges so natural,
they can't be contained.
I'm yearning to feel you in me,
totally and completely.
Go ahead…touch me…right there.*

Warm

I LOVE YOU LIKE
WARM CINNAMON APPLE PIE
WITH FRENCH VANILLA ICE CREAM ON TOP...
WE JUST MASH WELL TOGETHER
AND SO, I CAN'T TRAVEL ON THESE PARALLEL LINES
TIP TOEING ABOUT DISSATISFIED
AS I WAIT FOR A MOMENT AT MIDNIGHT
FOR OUR SOULS TO INTERTWINE
SO TIGHT THAT WE BOTH SUFFOCATE
UNABLE TO BEAR EVEN THE THOUGHT THAT WE SEPARATE
CAUSE YOU JUST FEEL SO WARM TO ME
I CAN FEEL YOUR BLOOD VESSELS
    CURLING THE HAIRS ALL OVER
MY BODILY PHYSIOLOGY
OF ME TRYING TO GET INSIDE OF YOU
SO YOU CAN GET INSIDE OF ME ...
'CAUSE TRUTH IS, WE'RE JUST TOO DEEP
I CATCH GLIMPSES FROM OUTSIDERS
    TRYING TO CONCEIVE
WHAT WE BELIEVE WHAT WE RECEIVE...
IT'S THIS LITTLE-KNOWN THING CALLED LOVE
THAT HAS THE ABILITY TO IGNITE FIRES, AND YES,
IT ENGAGES MY DESIRES TO TAKE OUR INTIMATE LEVELS
HIGHER INTO PSALMS, LIKE THIS RHYTHMIC MELODY
WHERE MY FRAME BECAME YOU HEALING BALM
WE PLAY IT CLOSE TOGETHER
MY SKIN IS YOUR VIOLIN
GO AHEAD, YOU CAN STRING ME ALONG

I'm almost gone...in your wind
We bind together into a perfect blend
of rising temperatures
Scribe me a romantic composition
and I will transform into pages
    of your literature
Cause for real I'm just into you
the way that Adam knew his Eve
it was an unexpected blessing,
    and what I'm feeling
is no less than the sin I'm confessing
perspiring from the touch of your caress and...
You just feel so warm... Tranquil... A serene breeze...
That got me stumbling down, knock kneed,
    unable to breathe
high off this ecstasy 'cause you touch me like
sunlight
and I promise, that I will bite into your
warm succulent juices of love
    that melt me all over
as I indulge in you like a spiritual Casanova
I get engulfed in your embrace
and I can't wait to feel the weight of your shape
on top of me as I surrender to you
    like God's grace
and all I'm asking babe
    is that you keep making me warm

Tatina A. Cowell

Come Close

Will you come close to me?
Just for a second, a moment
to inhale your fragrance
the nectarine of your sweetness
as I remember you warm and wet
Your ooohs and ahhhs
playing repeatedly in my mind
I touch myself reminiscing about you
your legs spread wide and open
My lips between yours lips
my sheets soiled in the essence
of your living springs
like waterfalls as your water falls endlessly
You slip off and on
off and on my tongue
Your thighs grip me tight
Your fingers ravaging,
tangled and locked in my locks
I let them lay loose for you
Now go ahead, play in my hair
while I play with you down there
I feel you, I hear you, spilling over
Fill up my cup with plenty of you
will you come close to me?
Just for a second,
a moment.
Please.

A Collection of My Humanity Expressed Through Poetry

Tatina A. Cowell

I Feel Like a Poem

Smoothie Dream

Is that peaches and cream
Or is that your special blend of strawberries
And tropical breezes dripping
    down your caramel skin
You taste sweet
You taste like Paradise citrus fruit
bursting and squirting with every
exotic motion of your feminine curves

I like playing with your lips
Getting myself tongue tied in a knot
    between yours thighs
with extracts of vanilla, pineapple
    and banana shakes
rolling slow over your clitoris root
And honestly, I think it's about that time that
I plant myself inside of you

So let's get cultivated

Your flavor is like
    my Tropical Smoothie dream coming true
And I'm definitely trying to make you cum too

Rolling my fingers around your clit
Watching you lick and nibble
as I get more stimulated by your tremble

A Collection of My Humanity Expressed Through Poetry

I LOVE SMELLING AND RUBBING MY FACE
IN YOUR LOWER SPACE, SO GO AHEAD
'CAUSE THIS ONE TIME I'LL LET YOU THROW YOUR
PUSSY PIE IN MY FACE
KISSING YOU IN EACH AND EVERY
RANDOM PLACE BELOW YOUR WAIST

I'M TRYING TO CONSUME YOU
SO WE CAN PRODUCE PRODUCE TOGETHER
INFINITE MEMORIES OR EVEN DREAMS OF ME
BITING AND CHEWING
CAN I SWALLOW YOUR TANGERINE?
CAN I SUCK ON THE JUICES THAT'S GLISTENING
ON THE CRYSTALS OF YOUR ALMOND SKIN
I WANT TO GET IT IN... SO WE CAN CULTIVATE

I'M THINKING LIKE, HOURS OF UNINHIBITED PLEASURE
AS I LAY AS YOUR PUPIL ALLOWING
YOUR BODY AND MOANS TO TEACH THIS LECTURE
LADY... I'M HUMBLING MYSELF SO YOU CAN SCHOOL ME

I'M TRYING TO TOSS YOUR SALAD
  THE WAY THAT YOU LIKE IT,
GETTING A GOOD GRIP ON YOUR COOL WHIP SKIN
  SO I CAN BITE IT.
I WANT FLIP YOU OVER ON YOUR FRONT SIDE
OPEN UP YOUR CHEEKS AND TASTE YOU
  WITH YOUR ASS HIGH

Tatina A. Cowell

It's coconut passion with my head
caressed between your melons
Plucking your nipples as you moisten
the sheets with your creamy dribble
I just want to sip on you!

But hey, it's like I told you before,
You're the flavor of my Tropical Smoothie dream
     come true
And I am most definitely trying to
     make you cum, too.

Make Love

I want to make love to you
the way that God created the earth,
molding and stroking every intricate piece
even down to the parts unseen
Tantalizing, kissing, sucking
every morsel of your frame
from crease to crimple,
from the curve of your hips to your every bend
I smile at the sight of your cheek dimples
I want to listen to you moan
as if it were the first breath
whispered out of the lips of man.
Though forbidden, I long to bite
deep down into your fruit causing
your juices to spill into an overflow of
love rivers spreading into bodies of
water surrounding our private paradise...

This is love making
as our intellectual and spiritual connect
to make manifest what's in the physical
Think of it like a sweet memory
of bodies aligned in perfect symmetry
My fingers pluck the strings of your violin
This is our duo symphony
Of melodic, hypnotic type of love making
that will send you into a trance
as your body continues to dance

I Feel Like a Poem

YOUR MIND FLOATING BACK ON
THE ORIGIN OF THINGS
CAUSE I GOT YOU DOING THINGS THAT
MAKE YOU REMEMBER…LOVE.

Play With You Like a Toy

Smack it
Flip it
Rub it down
Toss you up
I'll bend you down

Your body like play dough in my hands
Straddling you naked
I call you my little pony
Racing upstairs in Barbie's playhouse
but Ken isn't getting in
You like being my playboy bunny
Wrestling on red silk sheets
We're champions in this WWE
And Maybe I'll fulfill Your fantasy
and let you tag team me
but don't tag her in yet
'Cause I'm not finish getting you wet

Oh yeah, you knew you wanted to fuck me today
because you can't get enough of the way
    that I play
Like a toy meant for pleasure
and 'Tis the season of fucking on repeat
but you don't have to look for me
    underneath any tree
and we both know we're not getting any sleep
'Cause I got that toddler energy

I Feel Like a Poem

IS IT OKAY IF I CALL YOU MOMMY?

LET ME PLAY WITH YOU LIKE A TOY
TICKLE YOUR FUNNY BONE
LIFT YOUR THIGHS, OPEN 'EM WIDE
I GET SO DAMN TURN'T AT THE SOUND OF YOUR MOAN

YOUR CURVES, NIPPLES, HIPS AND LIPS
    ARE MY PLAYGROUND
I DON'T MIND CHASING YOU AROUND
TRAVELING ROUTE 69
I MEAN THAT'S OUR FAVORITE SPOT DOWNTOWN
I FOUND YOUR SPOT WITH A CAPITAL G
YOU SQUIRTING...WATER PARKS
GIRL YOU DONE TOOK ME TO *OCEAN BREEZE*
I WANNA SMASH
LEAN OVER SO I SMACK THAT ASS
I MEAN FOR REAL GIRL, I'LL DO WHATEVER YOU ASK

I'LL ADMIT I CAN BE A LITTLE CHILDISH
BECAUSE I JUST ENJOY
TAKING MY TIME AND
PLAYING WITH YOU LIKE A TOY

Sweeter

The door opened and I walked in
I was trying my best to wait patiently
for the sexual escapades to begin
I mean, we've been anticipating [together]
all day for our desire to sin...
For our chance to get it in

See, I keep remembering the first time
    that our bodies met
We were embracing one another chest to chest,
or as I should say, it was from breast to breast
Seemed like hours went by as our lips did the rest
to make every low down dirty,
    nasty thought manifest

She loosened up her belt and
I dipped my fingers in and felt it
Then she looked at me with a seducing grin
and said "go ahead babe, smell it"

Her fragrance, it ignited every sweet
    memory of me
sipping down real slow on the juices of
    her inner sea
Warm and moist her walls were spread
    all over my mouth
And yes, baby girl is passed aroused
Eyes rolled back, biting her lower lip
Trying not to shout

I Feel Like a Poem

But you know it's tempting, attempting
not to awake her man in the other room
Yet every time we meet, I remind her that dude
forgot how to do what lovers do

He may have mastered how to make her sweat
but he failed to remember the ways to make
her mind, body, and spirit connect
and yet he can't comprehend that it's me
the girl next door making his lady's pussy
and his new sofa wet... Oh yeah! It's like that!

Fuck a *Tonka*! I don't need a damn toy...
Because I can go deep,
but my fingers can go deeper
my tongue can go deeper,
and all the while, baby girl it's your taste inside
That's just getting sweeter

The Wet Poem

I can see her coming for me
But for real that girl ain't ready
She been nibbling, trembling for that
Touch, but before I lay a hand
I gotta get that mind fucked.
She asked "Can I caress that?" Huh!
She asked me "Can I get it wet?"
I smiled and said "Oh, I see you trying that?"
"Hell yeah I can get it wet!"

Now get your ass up on that bed
You know you gotta spread those legs
Lick the tip of your trigger
And let me watch for a minute
As your clit and tip mingle
Girl, rub it slow, then rub it fast
Arch your back so I can listen
To that moan blast
She whispered "Can I caress that?"
She said "Can I get it wet?"
I'm like "Oh, I see you still trying that!"
"Hell yeah I can get it wet!"

I got you remembering the last time
When my face was all up inside
I held your waist as your body whined
Oh really did enjoy this ride
Drooling down her walls
Tongue curdling up her spine

I Feel Like a Poem

'CAUSE I WAS GETTING THAT DEEP DINE
YOU ASKED ME "CAN I CARESS THAT?"
SHE SAID, "CAN I GET IT WET?"
"SHORTY YOU NEVER HAVE TO DOUBT THAT"
"HELL YEAH I CAN GET IT WET!"

FLIP YOU OVER, WATCH THAT BOOTY JIGGLE
REAL SLOW I SLIP MY FINGER IN YOUR MIDDLE
UP AND DOWN, ROUND AND ROUND
OOH, LET ME EASE BACK
CAUSE I CAN FEEL YOU SQUIRTING NOW
YOUR PUSSY JUICES ALL ON MY SHEETS
AND FOR A MINUTE, I SWEAR I COULD
HEAR YOUR TWOT SPEAK
IT'S LIKE TONGUES MANIFESTING
SHALALABOTAH...
YOUR PUSSY'S CATCHING THIS BLESSING
SHE ASKED ME AGAIN "CAN I CARESS THAT?"
BARELY ABLE TO SPEAK SHE SAY, "CAN I GET IT WET?"
I'M LIKE, "CHICK YOU NEED TO KILL THAT?"
"HELL YES! I JUST GOT YOU WET!"

Simple Satisfaction

MY TONGUE IS WAITING TO
CORRESPOND WITH YOUR VAGINAL WALLS
SLIPPERY WHEN WET
I SWALLOW HOLE AS YOUR
HARMONICA PEAKS
AND SCREAMS
FREQUENCIES OF HIGH PITCHES
AS MY SHEETS SOAK
AND I SLITHER INTO EVERY CREASE AND DIMPLE
THAT MAKES YOUR BODY SHIVER
AND TREMBLE IN PURE
YET SIMPLE SATISFACTION

I Feel Like a Poem

You Are My Words

YOU ARE MY WORDS...
I SPEAK YOU FLUENTLY
LIKE THE ANCIENT LANGUAGES
OF GOD SPEAKING LIFE INTO EXISTENCE
SPROUTING SEEDS THAT GRIP SOILS
OF PASSION FRUIT THAT SWEETENS
YOUR LOWER LIP AS WE KISS DEEP
DISSOLVING INTO LIMERICKS OF
INDESCRIBABLE SPEECH
YOU BECAME THE WORDS SLIPPING
OFF OF MY TONGUE AS MY TONGUE
SLIPPED INSIDE OF YOU
YOU TASTE SWELL
AND I IGNITED INTO LYRICAL FANTASIES
AS I SWALLOWED YOU WHOLE
I WRITE PAGES DESCRIBING YOUR TORSO
MY FIRST ESSAY I ENTITLED IT
THE WAVE OF YOUR CURVES
AS I FOLLOWED THE PATTERN OF YOUR FRAME
SILKY ON MY PALM. I CARESSED YOU WET
AS STANZAS BEGIN TO FORM
INTO CONSCIOUS LYRICS OF
CHEST TO CHEST...BREAST TO BREAST
WE NIBBLE ON EACH OTHER, NECK TO NECK
YOU ARE MY WORDS...
YOU ARE MY HAIKU
OF POWERFUL, SIMPLISTIC PHRASES
THAT REMIND ME OF THE COLOR
OF RAINBOWS PERFECTLY ALIGNED

Together into this poetry
I scribe you as you scribe me
On the scrolls of your heart
We become scripture
Inspiring the knitting of our souls
We intertwine into a single melody
And if I am the first line
Then you are the next that rhymes
With me
I love to write you so
That I can read you over
...and over again
...and again because
You are my words.

I Feel Like a Poem

PART III

I Feel Like …

I was made for this.
I was made to give it
But I was also made to receive it.
And I will not settle for anything less.

I Feel Like a Poem

I Don't Want You to See

I DON'T WANT YOU TO SEE
THAT I'M SEEING YOU
I KEEP IT A SECRET
THAT WHENEVER YOU ENTER THE ROOM
MY INNER CHILD STARTS TO LEAP
I AM UNABASHEDLY APPEASED
BY YOUR PRESENCE
I'VE MEMORIZED THE RAZBINESS
OF YOUR VOICE
AND YOUR SMILE IS EMBROIDERED
IN THE TEMPLATE OF MY MIND'S EYE
KINDA LIKE A THIRD EYE ENVISIONING
BEYOND WHAT'S PRESENT BUT SEEING
IN A PLACE OF WISHFUL THINKING
AND PREMONITIONS
I WISH I COULD CRACK YOU OPEN
AND READ YOUR FORTUNE
AND IF YOU'VE EVER BELIEVED
IN FAIRY TALES
I WOULD FIGHT LIKE HELL TO
MAKE THEM A DREAM COME TRUE

I DON'T WANT YOU TO SEE
THAT I'M SEEING YOU
CAUSE I GET SPELLBOUND
BY THE LIGHT WITHIN YOU
YOU SHIMMER KINDA LIKE
THESE TINY PIECES
OF CARAMEL CRYSTALS HANGING

IN THE CATHEDRALS OF MY IMAGINATION
YOU ILLUMINATE MY ATMOSPHERE
BLINDING ME WITH YOUR SHEER RADIANCE
I'M IN AWE…SPEECHLESS
AND SOMETIMES JUST DOWNRIGHT GIDDY

I DON'T WANT YOU TO SEE
THAT I AM SEEING YOU
I DON'T WANT YOU TO SEE THAT MY ARMS
ARE ALWAYS WRAPPED AROUND YOU
WHISPERING CONSISTENTLY AND PERSISTENTLY
IN YOUR EAR ABOUT YOUR WONDER
SOMETIMES YOU MAKE ME STUTTER
STUMBLING OVER MY WORDS,
OVER MYSELF… I FEEL LIKE I'M ABOUT TO FALL
INTO SOMETHING UNEXPECTED
IT CREPT UP ON ME
AND IT'S JUST PROBABLY JUST AN INFATUATION
BUT IT REEMERGES EVERY TIME AND
THE LITTLE KID INSIDE JUST RUNS AND HIDE
BECAUSE I DON'T WANT YOU TO SEE
THAT I JUST TRULY LOVE SEEING YOU

I Feel Like a Poem

A Collection of My Humanity Expressed Through Poetry

Her

SHE WAS...
MIRACULOUS
HER RADIANCE
WAS BEYOND MY WILDEST DREAM
WE KISSED
AND IT SEEMED
AS IF THE WORLD
SIMPLY STOOD STILL
FOR US

I... GOT...LOST...
IN YOU
MY HEART SWINDLED AWAY
LIKE A TREASURE
HIDDEN IN STONE
BLOOD, SWEAT AND TEARS
POURED OUT FOR ITS RELEASE
BUT YOU WERE WORTHY
YOUR SMILE
REMINISCENT OF RAINBOWS
I'D FOLLOW YOU ENDLESSLY
THROUGH PATHS THAT MAY
LEAD TO NOWHERE,
YET NOWHERE
IS WELCOMED
IF LEADS ME BACK INTO
YOUR ARMS
TIGHTLY HELD TO THE POINT
OF NO BREATH

Tatina A. Cowell

NO AIR
I INHALE YOU
WE BREATHE DEEP
DIVING INTO WATERS
SOARING IN AND OUT
RAPID WAVES AS
OUR SOULS INTERTWINE
INTO A SINGLE ELEMENT
WE FIND PEACE IN
EACH OTHER'S EYES
I CANNOT TELL YOU
A LIE...
I'M IN IT...
THIS THING WRITTEN IN
FAIRY TALES
WHERE CASTLES AND CROWNS
SHIMMER IN THE
CRYSTALLINE OF YOUR SKIN

YOU...ARE... HER...
A LOVE GAINED,
A LOVE LOST,
A LOVE REDISCOVERED
FOR YOU ARE THE ELEMENT
OF MY SURPRISE

YOU... ARE...HER

Melt

WHAT MAKES YOUR HEART MELT?
HONESTLY, I WISH IT WERE ME.

I IMAGINE THAT YOU
ILLUMINATE INSIDE
WHENEVER I WALK INTO THE ROOM
YOU RUN...
AND NO ONE IN YOUR PATH
MATTERS EXCEPT ME
AND SO, I CATCH YOU
AS FAST AS I CAN
BEFORE YOU STUMBLE
YOUR BODY FALLS PRECISELY
IN MY ARMS WITH A PERFECT GRASP
I CAN FEEL THE VIBRATION OF YOUR HEART
EACH BEAT ALIGNED
HARMONIOUSLY WITH MINE
A TEAR SLIGHTLY FORMED
YOUR PUPILS WET WITH
THE OVER ENJOYMENT OF US,
AND IN THIS MOMENT, WE ARE ONE
AND I MUST SAY,
YOU ARE AS BEAUTIFUL
AS THE DAY WE MET.

THE CROWD,
WHILE THEY EXIST IN THIS ROOM
THEY DISSOLVE FROM OUR MEMORY
SILHOUETTES FADING AS WE

I Feel Like a Poem

GAZE INTO EACH OTHER'S GALAXY
FAR BEYOND REALMS
IN WHICH HANDS
THAT KNOW NOT LOVE
CANNOT TOUCH

I ASKED WHAT MAKES
YOUR HEART MELT?
AND YET IT IS ME
THAT HAS MELTED INTO YOU

Life Like A Movie

TAKE 1
WE MEET
WE TALK
AN INCITING INCIDENT OF
INTIMATE CONVERSATIONS
TRUST INSTANTANEOUSLY DEFINED
BY OUR CHARACTERS' ABILITY
TO JUST BE OURSELVES

TAKE 2
AND IN ONE UNEXPECTED MOMENT
WE SHARED A MOMENT BEYOND THE PAGES
BREAKING DOWN THE FOURTH WALL
WHERE WORDS TRANSLATE INTO ACTION
SOME MIGHT CALL PASSION
IN THIS DIRECTOR'S CUT
OF UNCENSORED THRILLS AND CHILLS
MOVING THE STORY FORWARD

TAKE 69
WITH AN UNSCRIPTED
TURN OF EVENTS IMPRINTED
ON MY MIND
LIKE MY FAVORITE FILM
WHEN TIME AFTER TIME
I CAN REPEAT EVERY LINE
BUT NOW WE'RE ANXIOUS
FINDING ANY REASON TO SEE ONE ANOTHER
DINNER, A MOVIE, A DRINK
WE REWRITE THE SCENE

Tatina A. Cowell

DEVELOPING INTO A FULL SEQUENCE
OF DRAMA SURPASSING DIALOGUE
SCRIBED IN THE DIALECT OF FLESH AND SWEAT

WE LIVE LIFE LIKE AN EPISODIC THEME
AND I CAN'T TAKE MY EYES OFF THE SCREEN

I NOMINATE YOU FOR
AN ACADEMY AWARD FOR THE BEST LOVER
AND WHEN THE SHOW ENDS,
CREDITS ROLL SUBLIMINALLY
ENCRYPTED WITH THE PHRASE
THAT I LOVE HER... IN REAL LIFE

AND SO, I CAN'T CHANGE THIS CHANNEL
WITHOUT RUINING A PERFECT ENDING
OF A ROMANTIC, NOT SO MUCH OF COMEDY
WHERE WE GO ON HAPPILY EVER AFTER
I MISS THOSE TIMES WHEN WE USE TO CHATTER
ENWRAPPED IN THIS GLORIOUS LAUGHTER
HOWEVER, WE ENDORSED
      THE COMPLICATIONS OF THE PLOT
FORCING US TOWARD THE CLIMAX
AND NOW, WE'RE UNABLE TO AVOID THIS CONCLUSION
THAT THERE WILL BE NO RESOLUTION
BECAUSE WE COULD NEVER BE
AND I JUST HAVE TO ACCEPT THAT THIS LIFE
IS ABSOLUTELY NOTHING LIKE A MOVIE

A Collection of My Humanity Expressed Through Poetry

Loving You

Every morning that I awake
I am in love with you.

I love you for the person that you are,
I love you for the person you are becoming.
I love you for the words you speak
and the ones you keep inside.
I love you for your smile
and your ability to brighten up my day.

I love you in spite of your imperfections
Because you love me in spite of mine.

These Feelings within myself run so deep
That sometimes I fail to realize
Just how much I am in love with you.

I love the beauty in your eyes
and the sweetness of your kiss,
The caress of your gentle touch every time
our bodies meet

It's funny because I love you
But I have yet to find you
The one whom I will love totally and completely,
The one who will love me the same
Without limits or hesitation
So, I keep these emotions bottled inside,

I Feel Like a Poem

BOILING OVER UNTIL THAT MOMENT WHEN I DISCOVER THE ONE WHOM I ALREADY LOVE.

THESE FEELINGS WON'T BE NEW
NOR WILL THEY BE STRANGE TO EITHER OF US
BECAUSE WE ARE ALREADY PREDESTINED TO BE…

TOTALLY AND COMPLETELY IN LOVE.

She Likes Me

Oh, I hope she likes me
I get excited and giddy in her presence
I think maybe it's her essence
One she can't even explain
If I could define her in a word,
I would say that she's memorable
and enticing
Ooh, I used more than one word
But I just can't help myself
She's prissy and ole' so pretty
Her smile imprinted in my thinking
Oh, what am I thinking?
Oh gosh, I hope she likes me
I wish I could tell her how it is for me to rest
Because I just think of her as the best...
thing around
Capitalizing letters emphasizing
how captivating, I'm aspirating
just from an image in her profile
I know it's wild...
feeling a chick like this
and I'm doing the best I can to resist
but fighting almost seems senseless
yet I need to end this
Infatuation

I Feel Like a Poem

Oh, how I wished she liked me

But I know the truth
She's one I can never have
And thus far no one can compare
Because I see her as just rare
A precious commodity
Light on her feet
It's like she floats to me
Angelic, awe inspiring
Wow! She inspires me
Oh, how I wish that she liked me

Temporary Necessities

It was only temporary
what you gave me
yet in the moment
it was the thing I needed
though it showed me
My desire for more
More than what you could give
I uncovered the necessity
to be valued and not used
and while I'm sure
motives at one time were pure
the position of the heart
was never removed
It remained steady
rooted in hurt, possible voids
the necessity to be
needed, wanted…searching
for something permanent
in places you were only committed to
just for the moment
The temporary necessities
you provided me I will never forget
for they taught me, they built me
Strengthened me to know that
I am more than just being
good enough for the moment

Beautiful Sense

I make beautiful sense
I cause wildflowers to be meek
And mild-mannered,
They bow down to my very presence
Title me an unexplained wonder
An existence miraculously concepted,
It's me, and I'm not simply a theory
But I am godly spontaneity
Made manifest, and yes
Because I make beautiful sense
I am the living breath
That leads you beyond
Mediocre thinking
I am that woman that summons
You to get up off the surface
And dig deep...
Dig deep into the ashes
Of broken into mended
Stolen and now retrieved
Torn down yet found uplifted
I make beautiful sense
I am walking art
Divinely crafted by hands of love
And my Creator
He nicknames me Tender Care
Envision me more than a dime piece,
But I am a diamond perfectly pieced
Together by His artistry
Formulating into the gravitational pull

A Collection of My Humanity Expressed Through Poetry

Of what He defines as glorious
and good
I make beautiful sense
I can make the doves cry
And the lyrics rhyme
I cause shattered phrases to transform
Into perfect sentences
They develop
Line by line into paragraphs
Novelized in adventurous
worlds to establish
something great.
I am the inspiration of stories
that have yet to be told
The author of tales spoken
out loud and I stand strong and bold.
I am a woman of substance,
of essence,
Of magnificence and wealth
I have been classified as
More than a conqueror
A she warrior whose
Fearfully and wonderfully made
And I don't mind swaying
Nor carrying my sword
Because when all is said and
Done it's in my God's eye
I just make all kinds of
Beautiful Sense

Tatina A. Cowell

I Feel Like a Poem

Full Figured Artistry

I'm loving myself
before the rolls are gone
Embracing my own
curves because
my love runs deeper than
your superficiality
I walk confident in
my thick skin, voluptuous lips,
and my winter warm frame
It's no secret
I am no old style
Coke bottle shaped lovely
yet no doubt
I am still a lovely
A fluffy figured beauty
Just call me Queen
A dime and maybe
my profit has been multiplied
as I am the product, the sum...
A lady to never be subtracted from
Unless it is by my choosing
And I choose me
A caramel complected
Fully figured masterpiece
Layered in values
and though you pretend to be in disgust
I watch as your temperance fades
falling into lust
with my robust...

Tatina A. Cowell

I Feel Like a Poem

Waste, wishing for a taste of this full-figured masterpiece

A Collection of My Humanity Expressed Through Poetry

THE FOLLOWING POEMS ARE DEDICATED TO
MY BEAUTIFUL ELDEST NIECE,
ASIA LIONETTA COWELL,
WHOM I MISS MORE THAN WORDS CAN TRULY EXPRESS.
THE ILLUSTRATION BELOW IS ONE I DID OF ASIA
"BROWN BABY" WHEN SHE WAS JUST ONE YEARS OLD.
I WILL ALWAYS LOVE AND REMEMBER YOU
BEAUTIFUL GIRL,
MY BROWN BABY.

I Feel Like a Poem

For Asia

I WAS AWAY WHILE YOU WERE IN THE PROCESS OF
CREATION.
I REMEMBER THE MOMENT WHEN GRANDMA
TOLD YOUR UNCLE AND I THAT OUR SISTER
    WAS PREGNANT...
FIRST, OF COURSE, I WAS ANGRY.
SURPRISED? NO.
THERE WERE SO MANY DOWNFALLS
    TO YOUR BEING BORN...
AT LEAST THAT WAS THE PRIMARY THOUGHT
SEEN THROUGH MY NATURAL EYE JUDGING
THE MIND STATE OF YOUR MOTHER AT THE TIME.
THEN MONTHS WENT BY, AND YOUR MOM GOT FAT.
YOU WERE GETTING BIGGER,
AND YOU GOT EVEN BIGGER WHILE I WAS AWAY.
I HADN'T KNOWN YOU YET...
I HADN'T EVEN TOUCHED YOUR CHEEK,
BUT I ENVISIONED YOU
IN MY DREAMS MY BEAUTIFUL LITTLE NIECE.
BEFORE YOUR BIRTH,
I LOVED YOU WHEN WE WERE SEPARATED BY STATES
AND NOW, EVERY DAY AS I WATCH YOU GROW,
I LOVE YOU MORE AND MORE.

RIGHT NOW YOU'RE TOO YOUNG TO UNDERSTAND
THE ACTUAL DEPTH OF WHAT LOVE IS...
WHAT LOVE MEANS, BUT I BELIEVE GOD GAVE YOU A SENSE
    OF SOMETHING

A Collection of My Humanity Expressed Through Poetry

BECAUSE OF THE WAY YOUR BEAUTIFUL EYES
    CONNECT WITH MINE
EVERY TIME I TELL YOU JUST HOW MUCH I ADORE YOU.

TO MY LITTLE NIECE, WHAT YOU SENSE IS LOVE.

An Apology

I received an apology today
It left me with this feeling of lost
It left me with nothing more than
that feeling of hatred
Nothing more than the anger
The hurt, the pain...
Full, still and stuck in the moment

I received an apology today
That can't bring back
the life that was stolen
An apology that can't breathe life
back into the innocence that died
An apology causing me to question motives...
Is it sincere? Pure? What's the agenda?
Was it created from your guilt?
Did you apologize to let you,
or them off the hook?

I received an apology today
That can't restore the brokenness
or fill this empty space

I received an apology today
That really doesn't do shit for me!
Can your apology rewind the clock?
Change the outcome?
Is there really a right time
for an apology birth out of tragedy?
One born from a trail of hearts left in pieces?

A Collection of My Humanity Expressed Through Poetry

I RECEIVED AN APOLOGY TODAY
THAT LEFT ME FEELING NUMB, CONFUSED...
SAD...SO SAD.
TENSE AND UNCERTAIN OF WHAT'S
    RIGHT OR WRONG FOR ME

I RECEIVED AN APOLOGY TODAY

Tatina A. Cowell

One More Time

I wish I told you I loved you one more time
I wish I would have hugged you one more time
I wish I would've had one more time
    to laugh with you
One more corny joke with you
I wish I could've watched you sing terribly
    one more time
One more time to see you dance all wild
and fall out on the floor
One more time...
I wish I had another chance to see
    your beautiful smile
I would have told you I'll see you later
    instead of bye
I wish I wasn't in this moment,
    wishing for one more time
I wish I would have seen all your
    dreams come true
I wish you would have gotten that job that
    you dreamed of...
That business that you wanted to own
I wish I had one more time to debate with you
about what to watch on Netflix
I wish that I would have known
    what I know now...
That one day I will have to miss you
That one day I'll have to cry for you
That one day I would wish that I'd have
    more time with you,

A Collection of My Humanity Expressed Through Poetry

BUT THE ONE THING I NEVER HAVE TO WISH,
    THAT I KNOW FOR SURE
IS HOW MUCH I LOVE YOU, HOW MUCH I CARE FOR YOU,
AND I KNOW HOW MUCH YOU LOVED ME
    AND CARED FOR AUNTIE
I'LL SEE YOU LATER BROWN BABY

Tatina A. Cowell

I Feel Like a Poem

Quiet Now

It's quiet now
You were laid to rest
And the ghost arose
Bodies once loud and loving
How they've just floated away
Haunting houses
Not near
I don't hear their voices
But their memories linger
Fading slow until there is nothing more
You see, they seem to forget the after…
When the ceremony ends
They cradle and crept, yet my pain ascends
They decimate after the ritual
Yet what's been shattered never mends
I rely on the loyal ones
The few
But not too much,
Trying not to ruin or poison
Their will,
No one wants to be a burden
Yet I can't pretend that the silence isn't heavy
I mean, it's just so quiet now

A Collection of My Humanity Expressed Through Poetry

PART IV

I Feel Like …

Worship

To love You is to live You.
Give to You, I breathe You.
I need You. Consume me.

I Feel Like a Poem

An Unparallel Love

YOU'RE ALWAYS ON MY MIND
YOUR FRAGRANCE INVIGORATES MY INNER BEING
IT'S LIKE A FRESH BLOOM, YOUR PRESENCE THAT IGNITES
MY INWARD SPRING TIME AS IT POURS FORTH
STREAMS OF YOUR RESTORATION AND
RIVERS OF SPIRITUAL PEACE
I DRAW CLOSE TO YOU IN MY QUIET TIMES OF SOLITUDE,
LOCKED AWAY IN MY SECRET CLOSET AS WE EMBRACE…
TWO UNITED AS ONE IN A CARESS SO PURE, SO GENUINE,
SO TRUE EVEN THE ENMITY OF THE UNSEEN HAS
    NOT A SINGLE CLUE
THIS IS A LOVE UNPARALLEL TO NONE
NOT BASED UPON INFATUATION OR PRETENSE,
BUT IT'S AN UPLIFTING ON MY INTERNAL INNOCENCE,
CONSUMMATING INTO WORSHIP AS YOUR DEEP
CALLS UNTO MY DEEP, INTERTWINING AS THE NIGHT
DESCENDS INTO THE DAY. A LOVE UNPARALLEL TO NONE
MY ADAM AS I AM YOUR EVE…YOUR SARAI,
AS YOU ARE MY ABRAHAM…A PROMISE OF AN ENDURING
NATION FOUNDED ON FAITHFULNESS
AS I COMMIT MYSELF TO FOLLOW AFTER
    YOUR RIGHTEOUSNESS
IN REVERENCE I BOW DOWN, NOT IN SHAME,
MY LIPS AT YOUR FEET, MY INSIDE EMPTIED OUT
ONLY TO BE FILLED BY YOU
A LOVE UNPARALLEL TO NONE
I CAN'T REMEMBER THE LAST TIME I FELT THIS WAY…
COMPLETE AND WHOLE, NOW AN INDIVIDUAL AND NOT

A SPECTACLE OR A PARTICLE OF SOMETHING
THAT WAS LEFT BEHIND, BUT FULFILLED, SATISFIED BY
THE TOUCH OF YOUR HAND,
    THE WHISPER OF YOUR VOICE,
THE GLIMPSE OF YOUR SWEEPING STROLL
FOR I AM IN LOVE, CONFINED
    BY A LOVE UNPARALLEL TO NONE

I Feel Like a Poem

Be Silent

TAKE A MOMENT REARRANGE THE WORD...
SILENT MEANS TO LISTEN
LISTEN TO THAT SWEET VOICE AS HE SPEAKS
    SOFTLY IN YOUR EAR
FIRST, THERE MAY BE NO SOUND AT ALL,
AND THEN IT STARTS AS A WHISPER
NOT VERY CLEAR, BUT STILL ALLOW THIS TIME
    TO BE QUIET
IN SILENCE, REMEMBER THE DAYS YOU DIDN'T HAVE SEE
REMEMBER THE TIMELESS MOMENTS
    YOUR LIFE WAS SPARED
REMINISCE ON THE SEASON'S PAST,
AND THINK ON THE SOULS WHO ARE NOW LOST
HOPING FOR ONLY ONE WISH,
TO SEE ANOTHER RAIN DROP FALL, BUT
    THE ONLY TOUCH OF RAIN
IS THE DEW FROM HEAVEN THAT LAY
    UPON THEIR GRAVES...
MEDITATE ON THE LIFE YOU HAVE BEEN GIVEN...
A LIFE THAT DID NOT HAVE TO EXIST,
BUT BECAUSE HE SAID LET THERE BE, HERE YOU ARE.
TAKE A MOMENT REARRANGE THE WORD, LISTEN
LISTEN MEANS TO BE SILENT.
IN SILENCE WE RECOGNIZE EXACTLY WHO GOD IS
HE IS THE PEACE IN A TENDER SONG...
HE IS THE GOODNESS PRESSED AGAINST OUR CHEEK
    IN A GENTLE BREEZE...
HE IS THE TINGLE OF SERENITY STIRRING
    WITHIN OUR SOULS...

In silence we may indulge in the comfort
   of our Master's arm
In silence, we are given a choice...
The choice to be haunted by the stresses
   of past mistakes,
Or the choice to rely on the power of God
   to erase nightmares away
If we just take a second to a minute at a time
   to be still, to be silent
We may hear the internal revival of salvation
Breaking the foundation of fear
   bearing on our hearts
Hear all that the Lord has to say to you
Rearrange the word...
Silent means to listen, listen means to wait
Waiting is to be patient,
And patience is to understand
   that God is always speaking.

I Feel Like a Poem

Boy Tina

INTERNALLY CONFLICTED
BY THE DUALITY OF
TWO SEXUALITIES
JUST CALL ME A MAZE OF
MASCULINITY AND FEMININITY
GOING BACK AND FORTH
IN ONE BRAIN
THEY LIVE IN ME...
HE AND SHE
BOTH KIND AND CUTE,
BUT BOTH DISTURBED
BY WHAT THEY FEEL,
YET CONVICTED BY WHAT THEY KNOW

I NEED A
TIME OUT TO JUST LIVE...
TO LOVE,
BUT HOW DO I LIVE AND LOVE
IF I AM NOT SURE
IF WHO I LOVE IS OK

EVERYONE OUTSIDE
HAS AN ANSWER
ROOTED IN SPIRIT,
RELIGION, AND OPINION
AND NO MATTER
WHAT I CHOOSE
I STILL FEEL LIKE I'M SINNING.

A Collection of My Humanity Expressed Through Poetry

And so who's to tell me
that what I feel
is wrong outside of God
who speaks through man
scribed in scripture
inspired by words
still written by faulty man

Yet this is what I feel...
That she's beautiful
and he's beautiful too
Still both attracting
the two sides
leaving me suppressed
by what was taught
as oppose to what was loved
So she and he, him and her
battle alone with God caught
in the middle still
feeling out of the loop
cryng out "Tina, I love you!"

I Feel Like a Poem

Eternal Love (A love letter to my First Love)

THE FIRST TIME WE MET,
I KNEW YOU WERE THE ONE.
THERE WAS SOMETHING ABOUT YOU
    THAT MADE YOU DIFFERENT FROM MOST.
I COULDN'T PLACE A NAME, I COULDN'T FIND A MEANING,
    BUT I KNEW YOU WERE RARE.

WHEN I THOUGHT I HAD NO FRIEND
    YOU STOOD AS THE BEST OF THEM…
FOR THAT ALONE, YOU ARE AND WILL FOREVER BE
    MY ALL AND ALL.

WITHOUT YOU, I'D HAVE NO ONE…
NO ONE WORTHY TO UPHOLD ME,
NO ONE TO CONSOLE ME…
NO ONE TO FILL THE VOID AND EMPTINESS IN MY SOUL.
BUT BECAUSE YOU LIFTED UP MY EYES I AM GLAD.

SOMETIMES, I'M OVERWHELMED
    IN THE EXCELLENCE OF YOUR EMBRACE…
THAT SWEET TINGLE YOU SEND
    IN THE DEEPEST CORE OF MY BEING
WHENEVER YOU ALLOW ME THE PLEASURE
    OF CALLING YOUR NAME.

I AM IN AWE OF YOUR MAGNIFICENCE…
YOUR LOVE, CONSTANT AND IMMEDIATE FORGIVENESS
    OF MY SINS AMAZES ME.
I NEVER HAVE TO BE ASHAMED TO SAY I'M SORRY,

A Collection of My Humanity Expressed Through Poetry

BLESSING ME WITH INFINITE MEASURES OF COMPASSION,
INFINITE MEASURES OF INTERNAL RESTORATION.

THE WHISPER OF YOUR VOICE CAST ME IN A SPELL…
SONGS OF PRAISES RINGING CONSTANTLY IN MY EAR, YOU
REFUSING TO ALLOW THE PEACE YOU HAVE GIVEN TO BE
TAKEN AWAY.

YOU ARE MY EVERLASTING, MY ETERNAL LOVE.

YOU ARE THE APPLE OF MY EYE, THE KEY TO MY HEART.

THERE IS NO ONE WHO COULD POSSIBLY STAND
    IN COMPARISON TO YOU,
BECAUSE YOU HAVE GRANTED ME LIFE BEYOND LIFE…
LIFE THAT IS NOT CARNAL BUT SPIRITUAL.

JESUS YOU ARE MY FIRST LOVE…
MY EVERLASTING, MY ETERNAL LOVE.

TRUTHFULLY, I NEVER KNEW REAL LOVE…
THE KIND OF LOVE THAT CONVICTS ME WHEN I'M
WRONG…THE KIND OF LOVE THAT SIGNALS ME TO SMILE
FOR ABSOLUTELY NO REASON AT ALL UNTIL YOU.

THIS IS THE KIND OF LOVE THAT WILL NEVER END…
    IT'S ETERNAL.
IT'S THE KIND OF LOVE THAT WILL NEVER WALK AWAY
NOR BREAK YOUR HEART, BUT IT MOLDS IT GENTLY BACK

Tatina A. Cowell

TOGETHER, IT MENDS THE PIECES OTHERS HAVE BROKEN, AND ITS FINAL TOUCH IS A TENDER KISS ONLY A HEAVENLY LOVER CAN GIVE.

LORD, I THANK YOU…I THANK YOU FOR BEING MY FIRST LOVE…EVERLASTING AND ETERNALLY, I'M YOURS.

Flesh

Lord, I have been trying to figure out
what it is that I have been doing wrong...
What I've done to hinder us?
But then, it came to me...
Everything I have needed to give to You,
I've placed it so many times in the hands
    of ones made of flesh
So much energy spent...
Hours upon hours of conversing and listening
Even moments of sensual indulgence,
Touching and kissing
All of these intimate moments,
    pouring out my soul
To individuals who can love me in a minute
And can care less in a second

My fault Jesus...
I kept leaving You and leaving You
Just hanging, but still You waited.
So many times, Your signals and warnings
You told me how much You loved me,
    yet still I found
Myself searching for what You had already
    prepared to give...
I was searching for it in simple flesh

I Feel Like a Poem

I DON'T KNOW, JESUS,
MAYBE I HAVE TROUBLE TRUSTING YOU BECAUSE I FAIL
TO TRUST IN MYSELF – HMM, THERE IT GOES AGAIN!
HOW DARE I COMPARE YOU TO MYSELF...
I'M STILL JUST ANOTHER PERSON MADE OF FLESH

A Collection of My Humanity Expressed Through Poetry

Forward

I LOOK FORWARD TO EVERY MOMENT
WE SPEND TOGETHER...
THE QUIET NIGHTS, THE JOY THAT THE MORNING BRINGS,
THE PEACE AS WE SIT SIDE BY SIDE WATCHING
THE SUN AS IT DISAPPEARS BENEATH MY WINDOWPANE

I LOOK FORWARD TO OUR CONVERSATIONS
EVEN WHEN I STRUGGLE TO GET A CLEAR CONNECTION
I LISTEN CLOSE IN HOPES OF RECEIVING PIECES
    OF YOUR INFINITE WISDOM...
NEW KNOWLEDGE, NEW INSIGHT
    AS I STUDY THE MYSTERY OF
YOUR EXISTENCE IN MY PERSONAL LIFE,
    THE UPLIFTING OF MY SPIRIT AS
I WAIT TOTALLY IN SILENCE AS YOU DELIBERATE
    TO ME YOUR PLANS FOR
MY PRESENT TO ESTABLISH MY WALK IN THE ETERNAL

I LOOK FORWARD TO THE NEXT MOONLIGHT...
THE SWEET BREEZE THAT ACCOMPANIES THE DARK SKY...
THE TWINKLING OF EVERY SCATTERED STAR
    TO REMIND ME
THAT I AM IN YOUR SIGHT A DIAMOND,
    RARE YET PRECIOUS
A SPARKLING STONE, DESTINED TO ILLUMINATE,
    YET ONLY FOR YOUR GLORY
THE CRICKETS THEY IMITATE A SONG HARMONIZED
    BY THE WINGED CREATURES OF DAY
TO REITERATE THAT YOU ARE THE SAME LORD

Tatina A. Cowell

I Feel Like a Poem

WHEN THE SUN SHINES AT ITS HIGHEST POINT
AND THE SAME LORD WHEN THE NIGHT
    FALLS DOWN TO ITS KNEES

I LOOK FORWARD TO COMING HOME...
I LOOK FORWARD TO BEING WITH YOU
    IN A TIME WHEN TIME WILL NOT END
TO SING PRAISES AND TO MAGNIFY YOU
    IN THAT HEAVENLY PLACE
WHERE I WILL LAY, ENWRAPPED WITH TEARS OF JOY
AS SHOUTS OF ADORATION WILL JUMP OUT
    FROM MY BELLY
I LOOK FORWARD TO JUST BEING THERE,
WITH MY GOD, WITH MY LORD, WITH MY KING...
I AM LOOKING FORWARD TO YOU

Home

The ad reads, "A mansion, white wall interior,
jewels and gems on the exterior...
surrounded by clouds, an originally designed
    driveway paved with gold
Singing and dancing in the streets,
    no darkness in sight,
yet endless moments of new and eternal light."
You see, I'm in search of a home
I'm looking for my place of peace and solitude,
which at times feels non-existent yet
    this I choose not to believe
because as long as there is a God
    there shall be serenity
and joy and all of these things that I fail to find
in a world outside of home
My safe place to rest ... to kick off my shoes
    and just be me
A nonperfect person in a nonperfect creation
    created by the One Perfect Creator
Home, a place I am looking forward to
    because as long as I am here on earth
I am only a person, an individual, a pilgrim in exile
    but only for a little while
This was meant only as a temporary shelter
You see Heaven is the place where
    I ultimately reside with my Father
who waits for that precise moment
    to take us all home...
There's no place like home!

Tatina A. Cowell

I Feel Like a Poem

    THERE'S NO PLACE LIKE HOME!
SO I LIVE DAY BY DAY WITH A MIND SET TO PLEASE HIM
I DON'T WANT TO ARRIVE AT THE FRONT DOOR ONLY
    TO RECEIVE A PENALTY
OR A LACK OF A REWARD
BECAUSE I FAIL TO DO OR NOT TO DO
    WHAT I WAS CALLED,
WHAT I WAS ORDAINED…
WHAT MY DADDY TOLD ME TO DO…
TO LOVE HIM WITH ALL MY HEART, MIND,
SOUL AND STRENGTH AND TO LOVE YOU,
    MY NEIGHBOR AS SELF
YOU SEE I WANT TO GO HOME TO ARMS
    THAT ARE OPEN WIDE,
NOT TO A LOOK OF DISAPPOINTMENT,
AND MAYBE THAT LOOK WON'T BE ON HIS FACE
    BUT IT WILL BE ON MINE
IF I DON'T DO AS HE NEEDS
    OR THAT WHICH HE UNDERLINES…
TO OPEN UP THE DOORS OF HOME TO EVERYONE ELSE
THERE'S ENOUGH ROOM TO GO AROUND…
    IMMEASURABLE SPACE AND DON'T EVEN WORRY
ABOUT WHERE TO LAY YOUR HEAD
    BECAUSE ONCE YOU GET HOME THE FARTHEST
FROM YOUR MIND WILL BE SLEEP,
    WELL, I KNOW THIS AT LEAST FOR ME
HOME…THE ONE PLACE I CAN CALL MY OWN
THE ONE PLACE WITHOUT WORRIES,
    UNNECESSARY BILLS
    OR SLUMLORDS WHO AVOID DUTIES

HOME...A PLACE OF CONSTANT SUPPORT, COMFORT,
    AND LOVE THAT'S EVERLASTING...
I WANT TO GO HOME, TO MY FATHER'S HOUSE
SO I LISTEN FOR THE SIGNAL, THAT TRUMPET IN THE SKY
WHEN FIRST THE DEAD IN CHRIST SHALL RISE AND HE
RETURNS IN THE TWINKLING OF AN EYE
TO LET ME KNOW IT'S TIME TO GO HOME

Tatina A. Cowell

I Feel Like a Poem

I Worship

I WORSHIP YOU…
I WORSHIP THE GROUND THAT YOU WALK ON

NEVER A DAY GOES BY THAT I JUST CAN'T
HELP BUT TO SEEK YOUR FACE
MY HEART IT ACHES FOR YOU,
MY SPIRIT IT LONGS TO BE WITH YOU…
I HUNGER AFTER YOU IN A DRY AND THIRSTY LAND
YOU WATER THE EARTH OF MY FOUNDATION
TO BE NEXT TO YOU, TO TOUCH YOU, TO SHARE
A SINGLE WORD WITH YOU CAUSES
THE CORE OF MY TRUE EXISTENCE TO UNFOLD

I WORSHIP YOU…
I WORSHIP THE VERY GROUND THAT YOU WALK ON

I CHASE AFTER YOU LIKE A LITTLE CHILD…
MY SOUL REJOICES, BOUNCING UP AND DOWN
FILLED WITH CONSTANT GLADNESS AND EXHILARATION
I GLOW WHEN I AM IN YOUR PRESENCE,
DREADING EVEN THE TAUNTING OF YOUR EXIT, SO I CRY,
I WEEP OUT OF DESPERATION AND SORROW
WHEN I FEEL OUR CONNECTION HINDERED,
THUS I PULL AND I PULL, TUGGING AND FIGHTING
TO CATCH AT LEAST A GLIMPSE OF YOUR GLORIOUS SMILE,
NEVER REGRETTING A SINGLE MOMENT
     OF MY PURSUIT OF YOU
IT'S LIKE NOTHING I'VE EVER EXPERIENCED…
GRACE…FAVOR UNMERITED, UNDESERVED

Love... never changing yet its kind,
tender, gentle...never boasting,
but compassionate and still...
All of the reasons why I worship
the very ground that You walk

Some might view me as insane,
drooling from anticipation
as I crawl down on all four
just to follow after You,
memorizing every step in Your pathway...
Footprints in the sand guiding me
to this eternal light
of my eternal life in You
I can visualize Your lips close to my ear,
whispering in that still small voice,
telling me how precious,
how beautiful I am in Your sight
reaffirming the fact that there is nothing
that can ever separate this union of us two

I worship You God...
I worship the very land beneath Your feet...

I listen for the clinging
of Your sandal strap as You walk
through streets paved with gold...
when I lose sight of Your appearance
I scatter to capture the silhouette of Your wings
in hopes of discovering You yet again in
Your absolute beauty

Tatina A. Cowell

I Feel Like a Poem

WHERE EVER YOU ARE IS WHERE EVER I WANT TO BE
TO BE WITHOUT YOU IS TO BE WITH NOTHING,
AND ALL THAT I KNOW TO BE ANYTHING RESIDES
IN THE REAL ONE THING...YOU

I WORSHIP YOU GOD...
I WORSHIP YOU...I WORSHIP YOU

Intimacy (In-to-Me)

INTIMACY...
I WONDER WHAT IT WOULD BE LIKE TO HAVE YOU
    IN-TO-ME
I CAN IMAGINE QUIET NIGHTS, SLOW MUSIC
    WITH ONE MADE OF FLESH
BUT I WONDER WHAT IT WOULD BE LIKE
    TO BE LOVED, TOUCHED,
CARESSED BY THE ONE MADE OF SPIRIT
HOW WOULD IT FEEL TO BE ROMANCED?
AND THE MORNING AFTER, WOULD I FEEL DEFILED
OR WOULD I KNOW THAT I AM TRULY LOVED
WOULD I HAVE TO WAIT FOR NEXT TIME
    FOR US TO BE ALONE,
OR WOULD YOU BE JUST AS ANXIOUS AS I?
INTIMACY...
I WONDER WHAT IT WOULD FEEL LIKE
    TO HAVE ALL OF YOU IN-TO-ME
WOULD I BE ABLE TO CONTAIN MYSELF
OR WOULD I BURST FROM THE OVER INDULGENCE
    OF YOUR POWER,
YOUR GLORY, YOUR MASCULINITY,
    YOUR SHEER BEAUTY AND ADORING PRESENCE
COULD I HANDLE THE ONENESS OF BEING NEXT TO YOU...
THE ONENESS OF OUR SPIRITS INTERTWINING
WOULD I BE ABLE TO SLEEP WITHOUT BEING CAPTIVATED
BY THE CONSTANT DREAMS OF LAYING WITH YOU,
OR WOULD MY DESIRES, MY CRAVINGS ONLY GROW
    STRONGER THAN I COULD EVEN IMAGINE

Tatina A. Cowell

Intimacy...oh, how I desire not to wonder,
yet to know what it would be like to have You
    in-to-me
to truly receive what You are willing
    and are already giving to me
to know the embrace of Your care
    without the doubtful thoughts
of it vanishing away, and to rest with
    the assurance that this union is eternal

Intimacy...
    I long for the moments to have
    all of You
    in-to-me

A Collection of My Humanity Expressed Through Poetry

"Coming to Him as to a living stone, rejected indeed by men, but chosen by God and precious, you also, as living stones, are being built up a spiritual house, a holy priesthood, to offer up spiritual sacrifices acceptable to God through Jesus Christ. Therefore, it is also contained in the Scripture, "Behold, I lay in Zion a chief cornerstone, elect, precious, and he who believes on Him will by no means be put to shame."- **1 Peter 2:4-6**

Living Temple

I...SAW YOU CRYING FROM A DISTANCE
AND IT HIT ME IN AN INSTANT,
AND WHILE YOU MAY NOT BELIEVE THIS,
    BUT MY HEART BROKE
I GASPED FOR AIR, MY INWARD MAN POUNDING
INTENSELY STRUGGLING AS I STARTED TO CHOKE
I RECOGNIZE THAT WE ARE CONNECTED BY A BLOODLINE
OF AN UNBREAKABLE CHAIN OF EVENTS
RESULTING IN A MUTUAL SALVATION
IN WHICH WE BOTH MADE A PROCLAMATION
THAT RELEASED US FROM THE BONDS OF DAMNATION
IF YOU FALL, THEN I AM ONLY AN INCH AWAY
    OF LOSING MY LIFE
AS WE BOTH KNEW AT ONE TIME,
    CONTEMPLATING SUICIDE
BEFORE RECEIVING THE MESSAGE OF CHRIST
IT IS PRECEPT UPON PRECEPT
ROCK UPON ROCK
WE ARE JOINED TOGETHER BY A GREATER PURPOSE

Tatina A. Cowell

I Feel Like a Poem

No longer do I, nor should you consider
    yourself worthless

I say this to you deliberately
For it is now my responsibility
To hold you in a place of accountability
While I pass this point of hiding my hostility
Toward the enemy that battles against the Body
Individually to rip us of our eternity

If you stumble fam, then I'll catch you
Never again will I let you
Get caught up into this mess you
Continue to allow the enemy to infect you
Because it is just this simple...
I see you, the way He sees you...
As His moving, hearing, breathing, being, seeing...
You are God's Living Temple

Lost

I'M TRYING TO FIND LOVE
IN A BODY THAT RESEMBLES MINE
IGNORING THE SMALL VOICE WHISPERING
IN THE BACK OF MY MIND "I LOVE YOU, I LOVE YOU",
BUT I FAIL TO LISTEN WANTING
TO FULFILL THIS PASSION IN MY FLESH
THAT WOULD ONLY BE TEMPORAL AND DISSATISFIED
NEVER REALIZING THAT WHAT I'M TRULY MISSING
IS AN EMBRACE THAT HOLDS ME A PLACE
    THAT NEVER DIES
I'M TRYING TO FIND SOMETHING
THAT WOULD FILL THIS VOID…
AFFECTION…
A CARESS, A HUG,…
SOME KIND OF WARMTH IN THE ARMS OF ANOTHER
I'M SEARCHING FOR SOMETHING THAT'S REAL
SOMETHING THAT EXIST NOT SIMPLY FOR A MOMENT,
BUT SOMETHING EVERLASTING THAT GOES
    BEYOND THE SCOPE
OF MERE IMAGINATION AND UNHOLY DREAMS
TO LIVE IN A FANTASY MEANS NOTHING
IN COMPARISON TO THE INDULGENCE OF REALITY…
TO EXPERIENCE A GENUINE TOUCH
THAT CRADLES THE INNER PART OF ME
AND STILL I HEAR HIM SAYING "I LOVE YOU,
I LOVE YOU" THIS TIME I'M TRYING TO LISTEN,
    BUT AM I RECEIVING?
DO I NOW KNOW WHAT IT IS THAT I AM FAILING TO FIND

Tatina A. Cowell

I Feel Like a Poem

BECAUSE IT'S NOT IN A CARNAL KISS, A WOMAN'S HOLD,
OR A FLATTERING WORD, BUT WHAT WAS LOST IN ME
I HAVE DISCOVERED THAT I MUST
FIND IN THE ONE THAT'S DIVINE

A Collection of My Humanity Expressed Through Poetry

Love Song

THIS IS MY LOVE SONG...
I SAY IT NOT IN A MELODY OF ANGELIC TUNES,
BUT I SPEAK FROM A HEART OVERWHELMED BY YOU

I AM IN LOVE WITH YOU JESUS...
MY LORD, MY LOVER, MY SAVIOR...
MY FRIEND...

INWARDLY AND INTIMATELY YOU TOUCH ME
UPON A BED OF ROSES, I LAY PASSIONATELY IN YOUR ARMS
SAFE AND SECURE ALWAYS,
LONELY, I NEVER HAVE TO BE
I LIVE FOR YOU JESUS, AND THIS I MEAN FOR ETERNITY
FREE, I AM ALWAYS IN YOUR PRESENCE,
FORCED TO BE NOTHING MORE THAN MYSELF,
YET IT IS LOVE YOU HAVE GRANTED
WITHOUT CONDITIONS THAT COMPELS ME TO BE
THE WOMAN OF YOUR DREAMS

THERE ARE INFINITE MEASURES TO HOW MUCH
    I LOVE YOU...
I CAN THINK OF INFINITE WAYS OF HOW
    I WANT TO LOVE YOU...
TO TOUCH THE HEM OF YOUR GARMENT
    WOULD NOT BE ENOUGH FOR ME,
BUT TO EMBRACE YOU, TO TASTE YOU, TO CRADLE YOU
NOW THAT WOULD BE OF SATISFACTORY

Tatina A. Cowell

I Feel Like a Poem

I AM IN LOVE WITH JESUS,
MY LORD, MY LOVER, MY SAVIOR AND FRIEND…
I REST ON YOUR BOSOM
IT'S LIKE A FANTASY I NEVER WANT TO END
YOUR EXISTENCE LIKE A RUSHING
MIGHTY WIND THAT EXALTS ME FROM WITHIN
THIS IS MY OPPORTUNITY TO EXPRESS WHAT IS TRUE,
THAT LIKE A PUZZLE UNDONE
I WOULD BE BROKEN IF THERE WERE NO YOU
AND I KNOW THIS MAY SOUND LIKE A CLICHÉ,
BUT IT IS YOU LORD WHO COMPLETES ME
AND THAT IS WHY THE WORDS TO THIS LOVE SONG
CONFINES ME INTERNALLY

I AM IN LOVE WITH MY JESUS…
MY LORD, MY LOVER, MY SAVIOR…
YOU ARE MY BEST FRIEND

A Collection of My Humanity Expressed Through Poetry

The Master of My Being

I have the power to control nothing
only to be controlled, not by any force
made of flesh, but by One who appoints in spirit
My walk is a walk of trust in which I listen
for the Voice that instructs me from within
to direct my outward performance
     and to make manifest
the existence of righteousness not altered
By mortal election, but determined by
that which is beyond simple humanity
He is the Master of my being
My Creator, the One who knows the truth
Behind my internal and external cries
While science may assist, it cannot explain
The essence of my identity pre-written
in the Book of my life's story
the final breath that I breathe will be
my exit into the ultimate reality not to be
rationalized by theory or false explanations
but the reality of my Maker,
     the One whom I call God
the Maker of Heaven and of earth, the One who is
the Beginning and He will be the ending of all
that surrounds me to one day found
anew Heaven and a new Earth
in which He shall remain as He is...
the Master of all beings

Tatina A. Cowell

Might I Have a Room?

MIGHT I HAVE A ROOM WITH YOU...?
A SPACE IN YOUR SANCTUARY
THE GROUND THAT I'VE COME TO KNOW AS MY SAFE PLACE
IT IS WHERE I REST SOLELY AND COMPLETELY IN YOU
MY PLACE OF PEACE AND SOLITUDE,
THE PASTURE OF MY FEEDING
I LONG TO REMAIN NEXT TO YOU,
I DESIRE TO ABIDE UNDER THE SHADOW OF YOUR WINGS
IN YOUR PAVILION YOU'VE OPENED TO ME
    A HIDING PLACE...
A PLACE OF COMFORT AND SUPPORT,
THE ONE PLACE WHERE EVERY THOUGHT
    AND EVERY FEAR MUST STAND STILL
MIGHT I HAVE A ROOM IN YOUR SANCTUARY?
MIGHT I SLEEP IN THE BED WHERE YOU LAY?
MIGHT I HOLD YOU THROUGH THE NIGHT
    AND YOUR FACE,
THE FIRST I SEE WHEN THE SUN RISES
MIGHT I KISS YOUR LIPS JESUS, AND RUB YOUR FEET
MIGHT I ALLOW, OR I SHOULD SAY, YOU ALLOW
    THE STRENGTH OF YOUR EMBRACE
TO ENWRAP ME IN YOUR HOLY WILL
MIGHT I LAY WITH YOU IN THE DAWN?
MIGHT I BRUSH YOUR HAIR AS YOUR FINGERS
    GET ENTANGLED WITHIN MINE?
IS IT POSSIBLE FOR ME TO WOO YOU,
    TO BE WITH YOU TONIGHT;

However, my truest desire is the rest of my life
I want to lose myself... my being, my sanity
    and my intellect in You
I want to be emptied out of every piece of filth
So that I might be infilled with every part of You

I always look forward to our meetings
I am expecting You soon...
In the meantime, I'll book us a room

Nature

It is a part of human nature to be wanted...
To be desired...To be loved
Yet so often we forget that we are desired
by One who is truly the Ultimate of lovers
A heavenly, yet intimate partner who is able
and most importantly, He is willing to caress
the most inward parts of our being
It is a part of human nature to long
    for an affectionate touch...
To be embraced and to be cradled by another
and never having to feel rushed
    or brushed aside...
Yet how often do we fail to realize that there is
One whose arms remain open...
One who stands waiting to hold you
and to love you beyond the measure
of what your mind can conceive

It is a part of human nature to desire
    to not be alone...
Yet once we discover the eternal bliss of resting,
trusting and loving the Creator
We allow ourselves the pleasure of climaxing
Out of the human and into the divine nature

A Collection of My Humanity Expressed Through Poetry

Nevertheless

It's new...
I don't understand...
I'm not ready...
What if they hate me...
What if they don't receive me...
I don't want to be out front...
I want to work in the background...
I don't have all the answers...
I'm not ready...
I can't speak...
I can't teach...
I can't remember....
What if I mess up ...
I don't want to...
NEVERTHELESS
I rest...
I trust...
I walk as You wait...
I focus as You unveil...
I find confidence, not in self,
But in that which You will reveal
I lay as You hold...
I pray as You listen...
I simply be as You do...
I grasp as You minister...
I drink as You fill...
I eat as You supply...
I receive as You give...

Tatina A. Cowell

I Feel Like a Poem

I HEAR AS YOU SPEAK...
ATTENTIVE AS YOU TEACH...
I SURRENDER AS YOU CORRECT
OBEY AS YOU DIRECT
AND I WILL PERFORM AS YOU SHALL PERFECT

Season's Grace

THE SWEET SMELL OF SPRINGTIME
AS GENTLE AS THE DAWN'S BREEZE.
GOD'S ARTISTIC TOUCH DISPLAYED
BEAUTIFULLY IN THE GARDENS...
SHADES OF BURGUNDY RED LEAVES...
GREEN, VIOLET, AND BLUE...
HIGHLIGHTED BENEATH THE HORIZON
OF THE MORNING STAR.

IT IS THE TIME OF SEASON'S CHANGE
WHEN THE COLD OF WINTER FADES
INTO HEAVEN'S WARMTH.
AS THE SUN SHINES
THE WORLD BELOW FLOURISHES AND SMILES
IN THE GLORY OF THE LORD'S MERCY.

THE TURN OF A SEASON
WE RARELY SET ASIDE TO PRAISE,
BUT IT IS A GIFT AS EXPECTED AS TEMPERATURE CHANGE
THAT GRANTS US THE MIRACLE OF GOD'S GRACE.

Tatina A. Cowell

Simply Because...

I LOVE YOU NOT BECAUSE YOU ARE MY PERFECT CHILD
I LOVE YOU NOT BECAUSE OF ANYTHING
    THAT YOU HAVE DONE FOR ME,
BUT I LOVE YOU SIMPLY BECAUSE I AM GOD.

I LOVED YOU BEFORE I REMOVED YOU
    FROM YOUR MOTHER'S WOMB
I LOVED YOU BEFORE YOUR NAME
    ENTERED YOUR MOTHER'S THOUGHTS
I LOVED YOU EVEN BEFORE
    THE MOMENT OF YOUR CONCEPTION
I LOVE YOU SIMPLY BECAUSE I AM GOD.

THE LIFE THAT YOU LIVE IS BY NO MISTAKE,
BUT BECAUSE I FOUND YOU WITH A PURPOSE.
I CARE NOT ABOUT YOUR PAST SINS OR
YOUR RECENT DISAPPOINTMENTS,
    YET I LOVE YOU IN SPITE OF
SIMPLY BECAUSE I AM GOD.
DON'T TRY TO FIGURE OUT THE MOTIVES
    OF MY AFFECTION TOWARDS YOU
DON'T ANALYZE MY METHOD ON HOW I CHOOSE
    TO REACH YOU OR
TO TOUCH YOU. I DESIRE CLOSENESS WITH YOU...
I DESIRE TO EMBRACE, TO CRADLE, AND TO KISS YOU.
I GAVE YOU THIS LIFE SO THAT I MIGHT LOVE YOU
    FOR MYSELF.

You know that I am a jealous God and
My jealousy only grows simply because you refuse
To love Me as I love you.
Don't question or doubt My eternal devotion
      to you,
I was committed before you the carried
the ability to even speak My Name.
My love for you has carried you this far
And believe that My plans
      are to carry you farther.

I love you, not because of anything you have done,
But I love you simply just because.

I Feel Like a Poem

Step into the Light

    (Companion piece to *The Black Hole*)

I'M STANDING RIGHT HERE ON THE EDGE
WAITING FOR YOU TO GRAB HOLD OF MY HAND
I WAIT FOR YOU OUTSIDE, WANTING TO WASH AWAY
THE FEAR, THE HURT AND STAGNATION
AND COVER THEM IN LOVE, COMPASSION, AND JOY,
BUT STOP PEEPING AND
SIMPLY STEP OUT INTO THE LIGHT.
MY ARMS ARE OPEN WIDE TO YOU,
I JUST DESIRE FOR YOU TO TAKE HOLD OF ME
AND RECOGNIZE THAT MY LOVE, MY HEART TOWARD YOU
HAS NEVER CHANGED IN SPITE OF YOUR IMPERFECTIONS
OR DOWNFALLS. THE OUTWARD SPACE SURROUNDING
THIS BLACK HOLE YOU HAVE ALLOWED
THE ENEMY TO CREATE IN YOUR MIND
IS WHERE ALL OF MY OPPORTUNITIES,
POSSIBILITIES, AND BLESSINGS AWAIT YOU.
BUT PLEASE, STEP OUT...COME INTO THE LIGHT
OF MY PAVILION AND REST
WITH YOUR HEART IMPLANTED IN MINE.

I feel like sharing a word of thanks...

    I WOULD LIKE TO THANK EVERYONE WHO HAS BEEN PATIENT WITH ME DURING THIS PROCESS OF WRITING AND ENCOURAGING ME ON THE WAY THROUGH.

    I'M GRATEFUL TO GOD FOR THE GIFT TO CREATE THROUGH WRITING AND DRAWING. ART IS THE ONE AVENUE WHERE I KNOW I CAN BE MYSELF WITHOUT THE WORRY OF JUDGMENT AND LACK OF ACCEPTANCE, AND AT THE SAME TIME IT HAS ALLOWED ME TO BE OKAY WITH THE LACK AND THE NEGATIVE OPINIONS.

I Feel Like a Poem

I feel like sharing who I am

TATINA A. COWELL, AFFECTIONATELY KNOWN AS "TINA" OR "TEDDY", DEPENDING ON WHO YOU'RE TALKING TO, IS A NATIVE OF NORFOLK, VIRGINIA. SHE IS AN UNDENIABLE CREATIVE MIND, AND A TRUE JACK OF ALL TALENTED TRADES. TATINA IS AS A SPOKEN WORD ARTIST, A POET, RADIO HOST, SCREENWRITER, DIRECTOR, PRODUCER, EDITOR, CINEMATOGRAPHER, AND VISUAL ARTS CREATOR.

TINA HAS HOSTED, AS WELL AS CO-HOSTED SEVERAL RADIO BROADCASTS, INCLUDING "THE WRITER'S BLOCK" BASED IN NORFOLK, VA. SHE WAS THE FOUNDER AND COORDINATOR OF "THE CENTERSTAGE" TALENT SHOWCASE. SHE HAS DIRECTED, AS WELL AS EDITED SEVERAL PROMOTIONAL, DOCUMENTARY AND MUSIC VIDEOS. IN 2014, TATINA RELEASED HER FIRST FULL LENGTH SPOKEN WORD ALBUM "WINDOW INTO MY SOUL" AND 2015, BROUGHT THE RELEASE OF HER FIRST SHORT NARRATIVE FILM, CLOSET DOORS.

IN 2017, TINA STEPPED IN AS EDITOR FOR THE SHORT FILM AGED OUT, DIRECTED BY MS. TOMEKA M. WINBORNE. TATINA ALSO TOOK ON THE ROLE OF SCRIPT SUPERVISOR DURING THE PRODUCTION. TATINA HAS GONE ON TO FILM

CAMPAIGN ADS FOR LOCAL POLITICIANS IN HER NATIVE CITY OF NORFOLK, AS WELL CO-DIRECT, CONSULT, AND EDIT FOR HER FELLOW FILMMAKERS IN THE OUT-OF-STATE, AS WELL AS THE SURROUNDING AREAS.

WITH A PROFOUND RESPECT FOR GOD AND THE BELIEF IN GROWTH AND SPIRITUALITY, TATINA USES HER GIFTS AND TALENTS TO IMAGINE THE WORLD.
TATINA IS PRESENTLY WORKING TO BUILD INTACMEDIA, A FULL-SERVICE ENTERTAINMENT/PRODUCTION COMPANY, CREATED WITH A FOCUS OF BRIDGING THE GAP BETWEEN THE ARTS, LIFE EXPERIENCE, AND RAW SPIRITUALITY.

I Feel Like a Poem

<u>colophon</u>
Brought to you by Wider Perspectives Publishing, care of James Wilson, with the mission of advancing the poetry and creative community of Hampton Roads, Virginia.
This page used to have many cute and poetic expressions, but the sheer number of quality artists deserving mention has superseded the need to art. This has become some serious business; please check out how *They art...*

Patricia Davis
Tabetha Moon House
Nick Marickovich
Grey Hues
Rivers Raye
Madeline Garcia
Chichi Iwuorie
Symay Rhodes
Tanya Cunningham-Jones
(Scientific Eve)
Terra Leigh
Raymond M. Simmons
Samantha Borders-Shoemaker
Taz Weysweete'
Jade Leonard
Darean Polk
Bobby K.
(The Poor Man's Poet)
J. Scott Wilson (Teech!)
Charles Wilson
Gloria Darlene Mann
Neil Spirtas
Jorge Mendez & JT Williams
Sarah Eileen Williams
Stephanie Diana (Noftz)
Shanya – Lady S.
Jason Brown (Drk Mtr)
Ken Sutton
Britt Gardner
Faith May Griffin
Arlandria Speaks (Faith Clay)

Kailyn Rae Sasso
Crickyt J. Expression
Se'Mon-Michelle Rosser
Lisa M. Kendrick
Cassandra IsFree
Nich (Nicholis Williams)
Samantha Geovjian Clarke
Natalie Morison-Uzzle
Gus Woodward II
Patsy Bickerstaff
Edith Blake
Jack Cassada
Dezz
M. Antoinette Adams
Catherine TL Hodges
Kent Knowlton
Linda Spence-Howard
Tony Broadway
Zach Crowe
Mark Willoughby
Maria April C.
Vanessa Jones
Martina Champion
... and others to come soon.

the Hampton Roads
Artistic Collective
(757 Perspectives) &
The Poet's Domain
are all WPP literary journals in cooperation with Scientific Eve or Live Wire Press

Check for those artists on FaceBook, Instagram, the Virginia Poetry Online channel on YouTube, and other social media.

www.ingramcontent.com/pod-product-compliance
Lightning Source LLC
Chambersburg PA
CBHW031633160426
43196CB00006B/395